TEACHER ①   £3·90

COUNTERPOINT

**Coursebook –
Beginners**

Mark Ellis & Printha Ellis

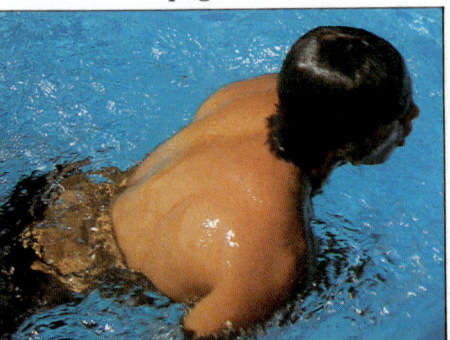

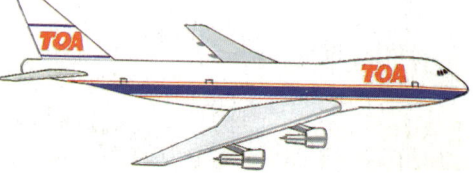

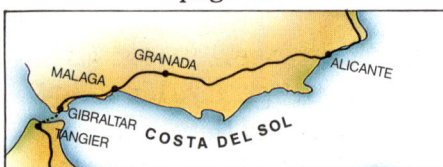

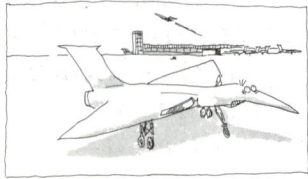

INTRODUCTION

Counterpoint is a new approach to English language learning which recognises in today's language learners a sophistication neglected by many other English language teaching materials. Counterpoint is a four-stage course which takes the learner from beginner to high intermediate level in 300–350 hours.

The topics and themes in Counterpoint have been chosen as typical of subjects which may be found in any general interest magazine or journal. The language is presented through realistic articles, interviews, advertisements, charts, and items of personal research.

Each stage of Counterpoint consists of: a Coursebook, which contains 45 compact units (including seven review units); a Workbook, which contains exercise material to practise language presented in the Coursebook; and Cassettes, which contain all the listening material, in the form of dialogue, conversation and some monologue, and some oral practice. The Teacher's Book contains lesson plans and extra suggestions for the teacher. The syllabus has been designed to follow a steady structural and lexical progression, which takes the learner to a good command of the language in four thematic stages:

Stage One: the learner as an individual
Stage Two: the learner and the environment
Stage Three: the learner and relationships
Stage Four: the learner and wider issues

Structures are constantly being recycled, not only in the review units, but throughout the course. The language is presented through reading or listening texts, and emphasis is placed on the learner's ability to understand and produce spoken English, though there is some reading and writing practice in each unit. The exercises are largely communicative and the topics promote genuine discussion and communication.

1 Ask and answer in pairs.
Are you French? (Belgian, Canadian, Italian ...)
– Yes, I am./No, I'm not.

2 Answer like this:

3 Listen to the tape and complete this form about Karl.

Name _____

Nationality _____

City _____

Now ask your partner and complete the form.

What's your name?   Name _____

Are you English?   Nationality _____

Where do you live?   City _____

Change partners and ask the questions again.

4 Ask and answer in pairs.
Do you speak English? (German, French, Italian ...)
– Yes, I do./No, I don't.

5 Choose a name from this list.

Johann, Marie-Claire, Mario, Juanita, Andreas

Now ask your partner:
Are you American?
Do you speak English?

6 Listen to the tape again and write what Emma says.
*I'm ____ . I'm not ____ , ____ American, I'm ____ America.
I ____ in New York.*

7 Choose a name and a town.

Names	Towns
Mary	New York
Pierre	Hong Kong
Peter	Madrid
Angelo	Rome
Su Lin	London
Pilar	Paris

Now ask and answer in pairs.
A I'm ____ . What's your name?
B ____ . Are you English?
A Yes, I am./No, I'm not, I'm ____ .
B Where are you from?
A ____ . Are you from ____ ?
B Yes, I am./No, I'm not. I'm from ____ .
A Where do you live?
B In ____ .

ARE YOU ENGLISH ?

1

8 Quiz
Where do people speak ____ ? Tick (√)

	English	French	German	Spanish
Germany			✓	
Switzerland				
Australia				
Canada				
Belgium				
Mexico				
Colombia				
New Zealand				
Tunisia				
Venezuela				
Austria				
The USA				

Make sentences like this:
In Germany the people speak German.

SUMMARY

Now you can :

introduce yourself
talk about nationality

KEY GRAMMAR
Question forms
Are you American?
Are you from England?
Do you speak English?
What's your name?

Where do you live?
Where do people speak German?

Present simple statements
I'm Swiss.
I live in Zürich.
I'm from Switzerland.
In Germany the people speak
  German.

Short forms
Yes, I am./No, I'm not.
Yes, I do./No, I don't.

Possessives
your

Vocabulary
be   yes
live   no
speak

7

ORIENT-EXPRESS COMPETITION

LONDON

PARIS

LAUSANNE

MILAN   VENICE

2

Win two tickets for the Venice Simplon Orient-Express!

Where are they from?
Put the letter under the city.

A   B   C

D   E

1 Talk about the competition, like this:
Where is A from? (B, C, D, E)
– I think she's from ____ .
I agree./No, I think she's from ____ .

2 Are you right or wrong? Listen to the tape.

3 Look at this chart.

name	nationality	language	town
John	Swiss	Chinese	Madrid
Ana	Scottish	Italian	New York
Michael	French	German	Turin
Claire	American	English	Strasbourg
Sue	Spanish	Spanish	Basle
Paolo	Italian	English	Hong Kong
Maria	Chinese	French	Edinburgh

The chart is wrong.
John isn't Swiss. He doesn't speak Chinese. He isn't from Madrid.
Where is he from? Decide and write, like this:
John is Scottish. He speaks English. He's from Edinburgh.
Ana is ____ . She speaks ____ . She's from ____ .

4 Now work in pairs. Talk to your partner.
I think John's Scottish.
– I agree./I think he's American.
I think Ana speaks Spanish.
– I agree./I think she speaks Italian.
I think Michael's from Basle.
–I agree./I think he's from New York.

5 Last year's winners on the Venice Simplon Orient-Express.

Nicole Dupont.	Rolf Schuhmacher from
Lives and works in _____ .	_____ but now works in _____ .

Listen to Nicole and Rolf on the Venice Simplon Orient-Express and complete the form above. Where are they from? Where do they work?

6 Ask and answer in pairs.
Where does Nicole live?
– She lives in ____ .
Where does A live?
– She lives in ____ .

7 Ask and answer. Use the languages below.
Do you speak English? (French, Italian, German, Spanish, Chinese . . .)
– Yes, I do./No, I don't.

8 Ask your partner questions. Complete the form.

ORIENT-EXPRESS COMPETITION

Name _____ Address _____

Country _____ _____

Nationality _____ Language _____

9 Work in pairs. Ask questions and fill in the gaps.

Person A	Person B
1 What's the winner's name?	*2* Where does the winner live?
3 Where does he work?	
4 What language does he speak?	*5* What language does he speak?

This year's winner is ____ . He lives in Mulheim and works in ____ . He speaks ____ and English.	This year's winner is Dieter Mann. He lives in ____ and works in Essen. He speaks German and ____ .

10 Fill in the gaps.
My ____ John. ____ work ____ London. I ____ English. Paulo ____ Italian and ____ lives ____ Turin. He ____ Italian ____ French.

2

WHAT IS IT?

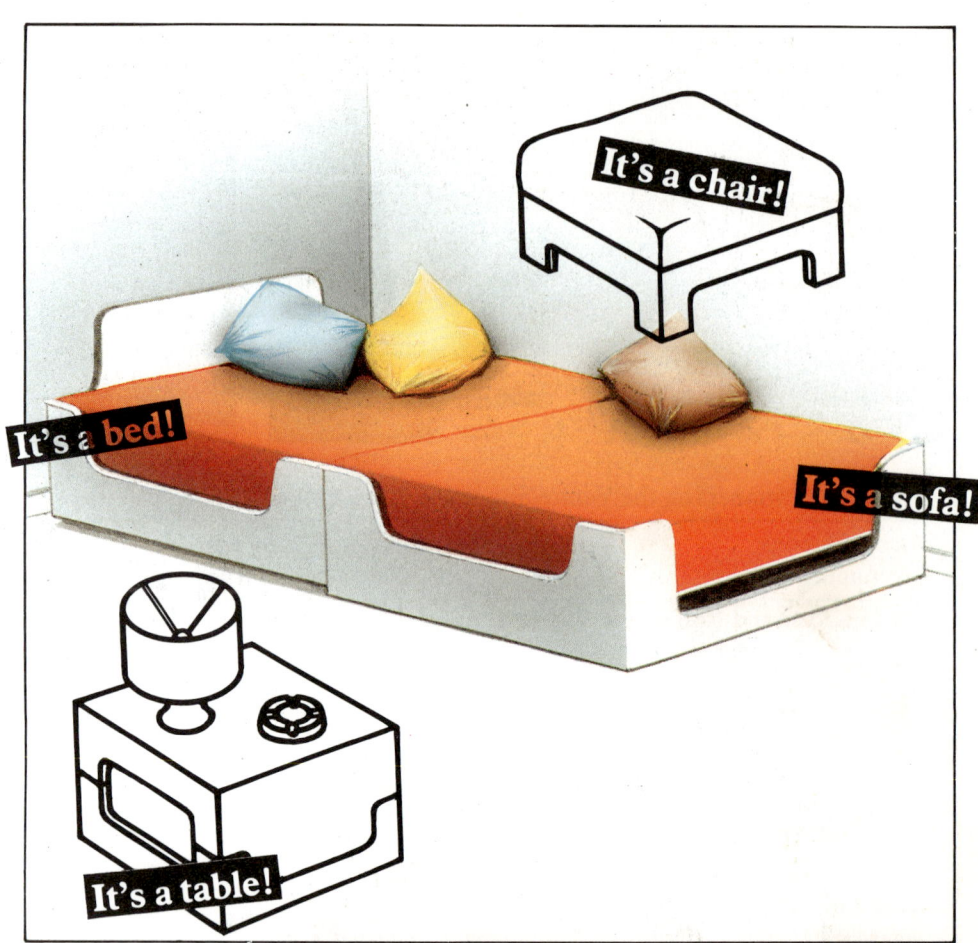

It's a chair!

It's a bed!

It's a sofa!

It's a table!

1 You work at Living Space.
Listen to the tape and fill in the form below.
Tick (√).

I'd like...

Living Space Order Form

Name _____

Address _____

Supalux towels

Colour	1	2	3	4	5	6	7	8	9	10
Red				√						
Brown		√								
Green	√									
White	√									
Blue					√					
Grey			√							
Black								√		
Yellow	√									
Orange									√	√

a	a wall	**n**	a clock
b	a window	**o**	a sofa
c	a chair	**p**	a cushion
d	a picture	**q**	pictures
e	curtains	**r**	a curtain
f	a light	**s**	an armchair
g	a table	**t**	a television
h	a tablecloth	**u**	a cupboard
i	a cupboard	**v**	a shelf
j	a glass	**w**	a light
k	a plant	**x**	a stereo
l	a carpet	**y**	a door
m	a ceiling	**z**	a floor

2 Ask and answer in pairs.
What's **a** in English?
– It's a wall
What colour is it?
– It's ____ .

3 Ask and answer in pairs.
What colour is **k**?
– It's ____ .
What is it?
– It's a ____ .

4 Ask and answer in pairs.
How do you spell **g**?
– T-A-B-L-E

5 Listen to the words on the tape and write them down. Ask and answer in pairs.
What's word number 1?
– Cupboard.
How do you spell it?
– C-U-P-B-O-A-R-D

6 Number puzzle
English numbers:

two four ten seven three one five nine six eight

Complete the puzzle with the numbers:

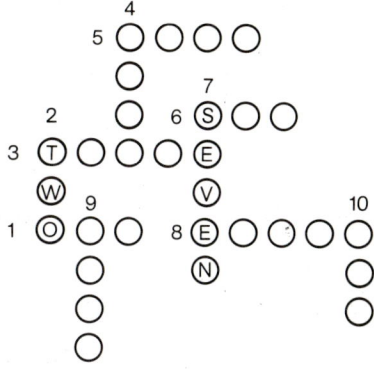

7 Ask and answer in pairs.
How do you spell 2?
– T-W-O

SUMMARY

Now you can :

spell
count to ten
talk about objects in a room
talk about colours

KEY GRAMMAR
Present simple with *it*
It's a bed. It's blue.

Question forms
How do you spell . . . ?
What is . . . in English?
What colour is it?

Articles
a television
an armchair

Vocabulary
spell
I'd like

FASHION PARADE

[handwritten annotations: Talking about clothes. "is happening now. I am wearing / He is wearing / she / they are } Present Simple - 3rd person singular - negative + interrogative]

[handwritten: Michel — pale blue — in blue; Janine — cream]

[handwritten: Alexei — purple]

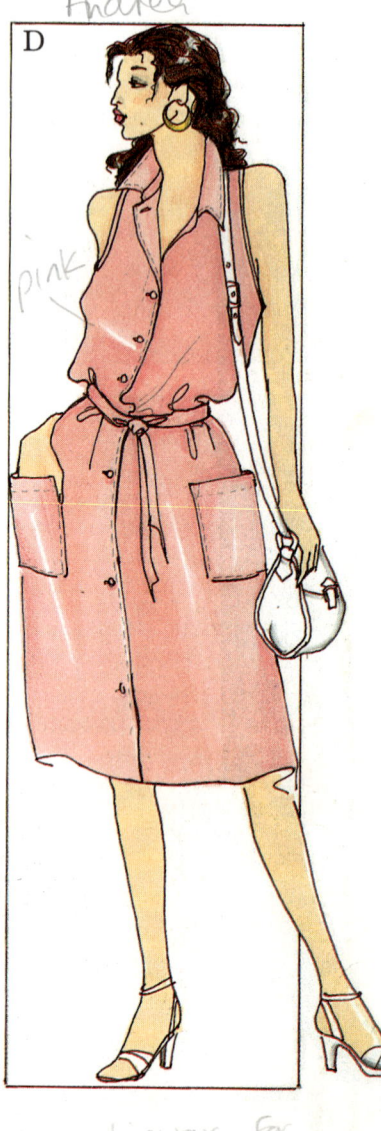

[handwritten: Andrea — pink]

4

[handwritten below images: Fashion Show | stress = handbag, jacket | sandals, trousers | Present continuous for current continuous actions.]

1 Listen to the tape and fill in the gaps.
This is Andrea. Today she's wearing a ____ ____ and ____ ____.
Her ____ is from the Caravelle summer collection. She's carrying a
____ ____ from Ecstasy.
This is Michel. He's wearing a ____ ____ ____ and ____ ____ ____.
He's carrying a ____ ____. His ____ are from Miracle.
And here's Janine. She isn't wearing holiday clothes this year. Today she's
wearing a ____ ____ and ____, with a ____ ____ and ____ ____.
She's carrying a ____ ____.
Finally, Alexei is wearing ____ and a ____ by Lisko. His ____ are ____ and
____ and the ____ is ____ and ____. He's wearing a ____ ____ and ____ ____,
and is carrying a ____. Very colourful clothes!

2 Match Andrea, Michel, Janine and Alexei with A, B, C and D above.

3 Ask and answer in pairs.
Is Andrea wearing a skirt?
    a dress,
    shoes,
    trousers
– *Yes, she is./No, she isn't.*
What colour is (are) her skirt?
    dress,
    shoes,
    trousers
– *It's ____.*

(Be careful – a skirt/a dress *is* but
shoes/trousers *are*)

4 What is Janine wearing? Can you remember?
Close your books and write down her clothes.
What is Alexei wearing? Write down his clothes.
Now ask your partner:
What is Janine wearing?
– I think she's wearing a black dress. Am I right?
Yes. I think so./No, I think she's wearing ____.
Then check your answers.

5 Choose two or three people in your class. Write about their clothes.
____ is wearing a ____ ____ and ____ ____. He/she is wearing ____.
His/her ____ is/are ____.

6 Now other people in the class guess the names of the people.
Give one clue.
He's wearing a shirt.
– Is it white?
Yes, it is./No, it isn't.
– Is he wearing black trousers?
Yes, he is./No, he isn't.
– Is his name John?
Yes, it is./No, it isn't.

7 Look at this sentence from the text.
Janine's wearing a jacket, a skirt, a blouse and shoes.
She's carrying a handbag.
Now write sentences like this:
– The jacket is brown.
– The skirt is brown.
– The blouse is cream.
– The shoes are brown.

8 Look up these words in a dictionary.

a footballer **b** jockey   **c** ice-skater   **d** boxer

Now listen to the tape and complete these words.

(i) c**a**p   **(ii)** sho**r**t**s**   **(iii)** d**re**ss   **(iv)** **s**hir**t**
sk**i**rt   b**oo**ts   sh**o**r**s**

Now match **a**, **b**, **c** and **d** with **(i)**, **(ii)**, **(iii)** and **(iv)**.

Write sentences, like this:
This is a/an ____. He/she is wearing ____.

SUMMARY

Now you can:

talk about clothes

KEY GRAMMAR
Question forms
Is Andrea wearing a skirt?
What is Janine wearing?
What colour is her skirt?
Is it white?

Short forms
Yes, she is./No, she isn't.
Yes, it is./No, it isn't.

Present continuous statements
She's wearing a skirt. The skirt is
    black.
She isn't wearing holiday clothes.
I think she's carrying a bag.

Articles
the

Possessives
his
her

Vocabulary
carry
think
wear

bag
blouse
boots
cap
clothes
dress
handbag
hat
jacket
sandals
shirt
shoes
shorts
skirt
sweater
trousers

boxer
footballer
ice-skater
jockey

4

Breakfast in New York, lunch in London,

What do they do every day?

Jennie

Jennie is a taxi driver. She gets up at seven o'clock **7.00** every day. She has her breakfast at eight **8.00**. She has lunch between ten past twelve **12.10** and twenty to one **12.40**. She has dinner at about six o'clock **18.00**. She goes to bed between half past ten **22.30** and midnight **24.00**.

1 Answer the questions about Jennie.
1 What time does Jennie get up?
2 What time does she have breakfast?
3 What time does she have lunch?
4 What time does she go to bed?

5

Lucy Wu

Lucy Wu is a tennis player. She gets up at about a quarter past six **6.15**. She has her breakfast at about a quarter to seven **6.45**. She has lunch between twenty-five to twelve **11.35** and twenty-five to one **12.35**. She doesn't have dinner at home. She eats in a restaurant. She goes to bed before eleven o'clock **23.00**.

2 Answer the questions about Lucy Wu.
What time does Lucy Wu
1 get up?
2 have breakfast?
3 have lunch?
4 go to bed?

3 Now read the following and complete the sentences.

Jürgen

Jürgen is a baker. He gets up at four thirty **4.30** and has a cup of coffee. Then he goes to work at five o'clock **5.00**. He has lunch with Gabrielle at one o'clock **1.00**. He works twelve hours a day and goes to bed at nine o'clock **21.00**.

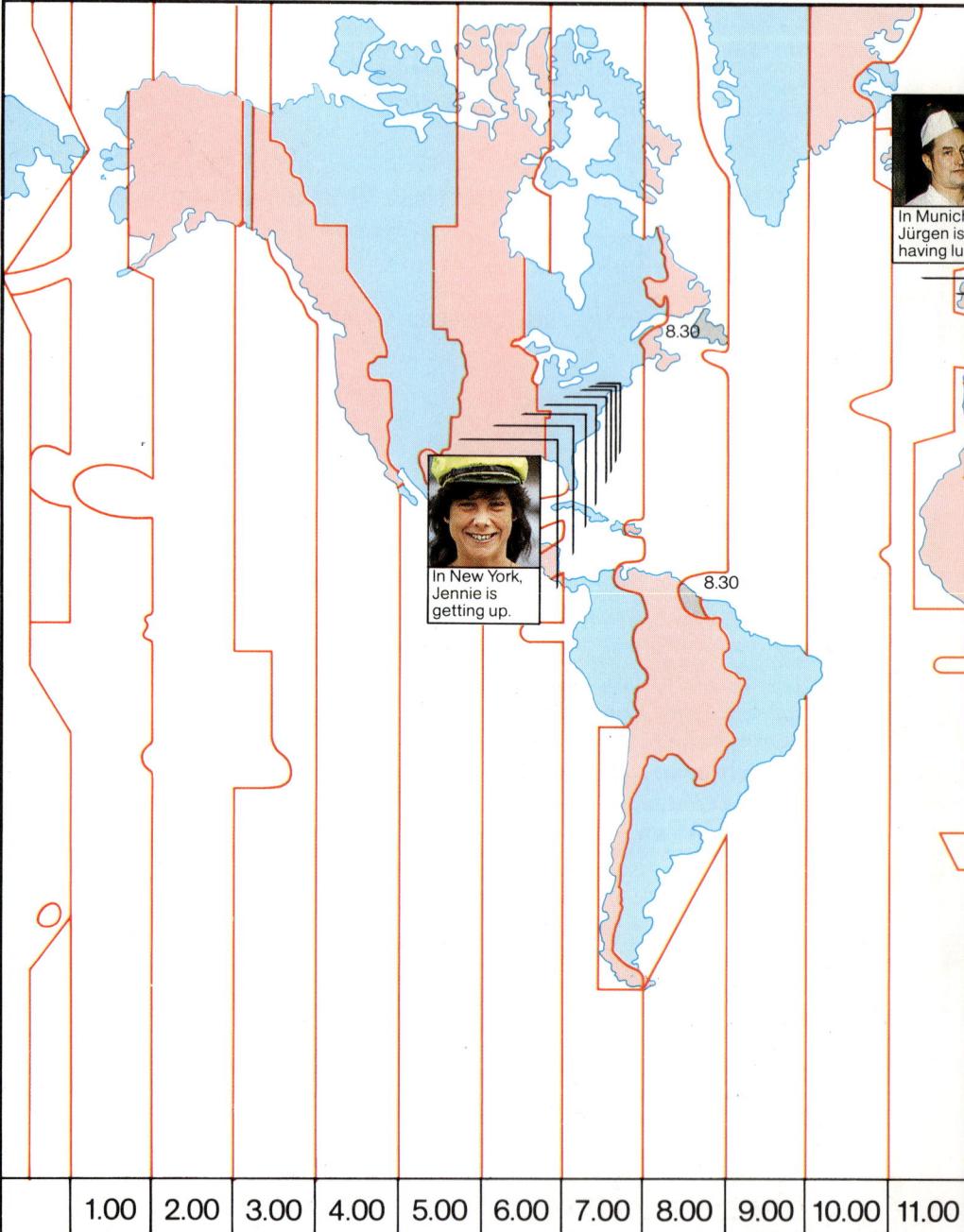

In Munich, Jürgen is having lun[ch]

In New York, Jennie is getting up.

8.30

8.30

1.00	2.00	3.00	4.00	5.00	6.00	7.00	8.00	9.00	10.00	11.00

Yushi

Yushi is a farmer. He gets up every day at five thirty **5.30**. He doesn't have breakfast. He goes to work at six fifteen **6.15**. His lunch is at midday **12.00**. Yushi goes home at five fifteen **17.15** and he has dinner after seven o'clock **19.00**. He goes to bed at about ten o'clock **22.00**.

1 Jürgen comes home at ____.
2 He sleeps ____ hours a night.
3 Yushi sleeps ____ hours a night.
4 He works ____ hours a day.

4 Listen to the tape. Gabrielle is in Munich. She is phoning Jennie in New York. What's the time?

5 Here is a phone call. Listen to the tape and complete it. Then practise it in pairs.
A Hello, Pilar?
B Yes, ____, who's speaking?
A It's Simon. ____ in L.A.
B Oh, Simon! ____ in Los Angeles?
A ____. What's the time in Madrid?
B It's nine o'clock here. Are you working?

14

dinner in Tokyo

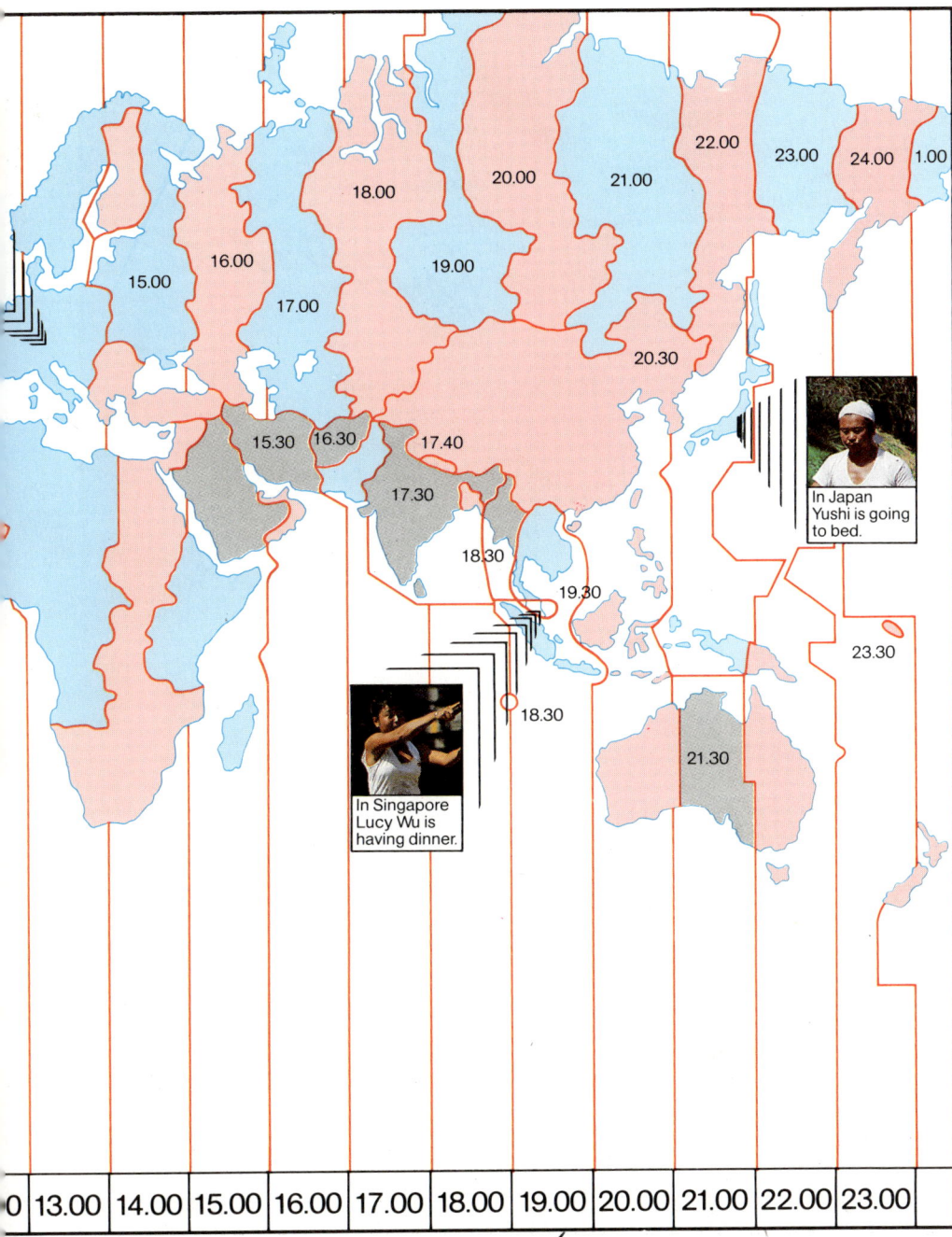

15.00 16.00 17.00 18.00 19.00 20.00 21.00 22.00 23.00 24.00 1.00

15.30 16.30 17.40
17.30
18.30
19.30
18.30
20.30
23.30
21.30

In Japan Yushi is going to bed.

In Singapore Lucy Wu is having dinner.

	13.00	14.00	15.00	16.00	17.00	18.00	19.00	20.00	21.00	22.00	23.00	

A No, I'm not. I'm ____. What ____?
B ____.

6 Ask and answer in pairs.
*What time do you get up? (go to work/
bed; have breakfast/lunch/dinner)*
– I get up at ____.

7 Ask and answer in pairs.
*What do you do at 7.30? (9.00, 12.30,
17.00, 18.30, 22.00, 24.00)*
– At 7.30 I ____.

8 What's the time now?
What's the time in New York?
(Munich, Tokyo, Singapore)
– It's ____.
What is Jennie doing?
(Jürgen, Yushi, Lucy Wu)
– She's ____.

9 Write about your day. *(in Treviso)*
I get up at ____ and I have my ____
at ____. I have lunch between ____
and ____. I ____ dinner at ____ and
____ at about ____.

SUMMARY

Now you can:

tell the time
say what you are doing
say what you do every day

KEY GRAMMAR

Question forms
What's the time?
Is Jürgen there?
Who's speaking?
What time does she get up?

Present simple statements
Jennie is a taxi driver.
She gets up at six.
This is Pilar.
It's half past six.

Prepositions
She gets up at six.
She goes to bed before/after ten.
… between one and seven.

Time
12.00 midday
24.00 midnight
11.00 eleven o'clock
11.05 five past eleven
       eleven oh five
11.15 quarter past eleven
       eleven fifteen
11.30 half past eleven
       eleven thirty
11.45 quarter to twelve
       eleven forty-five
11.55 five to twelve
       eleven fifty-five

Vocabulary
eat
get up
go
have (+ dinner etc)

breakfast
lunch
dinner

taxi driver
baker
tennis player
farmer

5

REVISION

6

Dear Carrie

How do you say ___ in English? In Hong Kong we call it a wok.
Thank you for your help.
Yours sincerely

Ah Poon

Dear Ah Poon
Thank you for your letter. In English it is also a wok.

Carrie

Dear Carrie

How do you spell ___ in English? I think the spelling is t-y-r-e. Am I right?
Yours sincerely

Gunther

Dear Gunther
Yes, you are right. The spelling in Britain is t-y-r-e, but in America the spelling is t-i-r-e.

Carrie

1 Letter writing
Write a letter to Carrie. Ask the English word for something.
Write another letter and ask the spelling of a word.

2 Match the columns
Ask and answer questions.
What language do the people speak in the USA?
– They speak English.

The USA	Swedish
France	Arabic
The Netherlands	Danish
Austria	English
Spain	French
Sweden	Dutch
Denmark	Greek
Tunisia	Spanish
Greece	German

3 Complete the words. *Putting in vowels.*
Here are some verbs from Units 1 to 5. What are they?
SPE_K = SPEAK

SPE_K   SP_LL   _S   L_VE

S_Y   _RE   LI_E   C_LL   H_VE

WO_K   WE_R   G_T UP   THI_K

D_   G_ TO BED   E_T   UND_RST_ND

Now write five sentences with five of the verbs.
I live in Hamburg.

4 Ask your partner questions and complete the charts.

My partner

Name _____
City _____
Languages _____
_____

Me

Name _____
City _____
Languages _____
_____

5 Time

Write the time, like this:

It's three forty-five.
It's quarter to four.

6 Who am I? What do I do?

Answer these questions about yourself.

What's your name?

Where do you live?

What nationality are you?

What languages do you speak?

What time do you get up?

What time do you go to bed?

What time do you have lunch?

7 Ask and answer questions about your classroom and the people.

What colour is the ____?

It's ____.

How do you spell ____?

8 Make words and sentences.

Ute – der trisk   Ute is wearing a red skirt.

Gabi – twihe bousle   Gabi is wearing ____.
Lise – uelb weastre   Lise ____.
Tom – nrowb hoess   Tom ____.
Rudi – lackb otsreurs   Rudi ____.

white blouse
blue sweater
brown shoes
black trousers.

Ute   Gabi   Lise   Tom   Rudi

MILTON KEYNES

7

new town 50 miles ? London ?

bringing people + industry from London into the provinces. Started in 1976 + popn. today is 117,000.

A NEW TOWN, NEW HOUSES, NEW FLATS

Practise the possessive adj

Drill : T. He's got a large living rm. St. His living room is large.

Milton Keynes is a new town and a lot of people are buying houses there. Here are five:

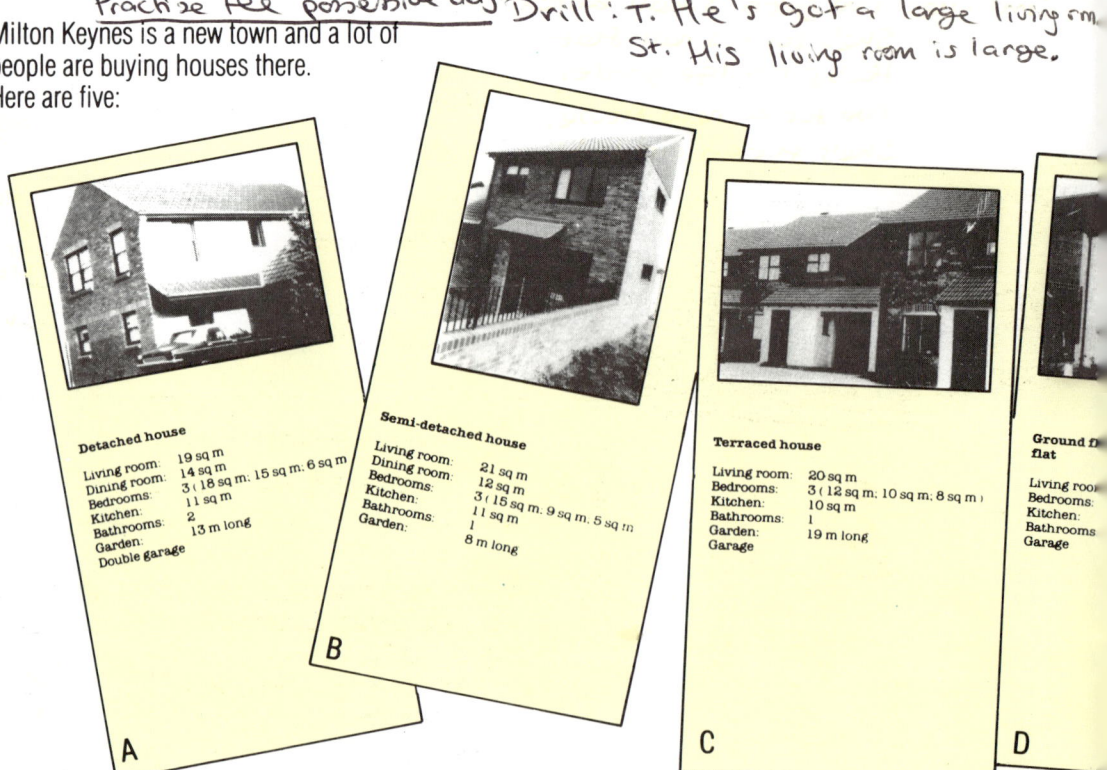

Detached house

Living room:	19 sq m
Dining room:	14 sq m
Bedrooms:	3 (18 sq m; 15 sq m; 6 sq m
Kitchen:	11 sq m
Bathrooms:	2
Garden:	13 m long
Double garage	

A

Semi-detached house

Living room:	21 sq m
Dining room:	12 sq m
Bedrooms:	3 (15 sq m; 9 sq m; 5 sq m
Kitchen:	11 sq m
Bathrooms:	
Garden:	8 m long

B

Terraced house

Living room:	20 sq m
Bedrooms:	3 (12 sq m; 10 sq m; 8 sq m)
Kitchen:	10 sq m
Bathrooms:	1
Garden:	19 m long
Garage	

C

Ground f flat

Living room:	
Bedrooms:	
Kitchen:	
Bathrooms:	
Garage	

D

Present Simple: There is ..
1) > have got. " are ..
2) question wds.

How many? .. large?

How many rooms has it got?
How large is your bathroom?

1 Listen to the tape.
Mrs Robinson lives in Milton Keynes. Does she live in **A, B, C, D** or **E**?

2 Jack Peters also lives in Milton Keynes. He's got three bedrooms, but only one bathroom. His living room is large. He's also got a large garden. His kitchen is ten square metres. Does Jack Peters live in **A, B, C, D** or **E**?

3 You also live in Milton Keynes. Choose another house or flat. Now answer your partner's questions:
How many _____ are there?
– There are _____.
Is there a _____ ?
– Yes, there is./No, there isn't.
How large is the _____ ?
– It's _____.
Do you live in a _____ ?
– Yes, I do./No, I don't.
Is _____ new?
– Yes, it is./No, it isn't.
Do you like it?
– Yes, _____/No, _____.

Say: *I think you live in _____.*

4 Find out about your partner's house and complete this table. (in England)

... A NEW LIFE

Continue: I've got a small bedroom.
She's got a small flat.
He's got a lge garden.
I've got a new house.
She's got an old kitchen.

21 sq m
2 (20 sq m; 16 sq m)
10 sq m
1

First floor maisonette

Living room: 15 sq m
Bedrooms: 1 (10 sq m)
Kitchen: 8 sq m
Bathrooms: 1

E

House/flat	_____
New/old	_____
Number of rooms	_____
Number of bedrooms	_____
bathrooms	_____
Size of living room	_____
kitchen	_____
bedrooms	_____
	_____
Is there a garden? (yes/no)	_____
garage? (yes/no)	_____

5 Choose a new partner. Look at the chart. Ask questions about his/her old partner, like this:
Does he/she live in a house or flat?
How large is the _____ ?
Is there a _____ ?
Does he/she like it?

Now you can:

talk about houses
use plurals —

-s   pron.
-es   57.12
-eys
-ies   irr.
roofs   child
sheep   man

KEY GRAMMAR
Question forms
Are they large or small?
How large is the kitchen?
How many bedrooms are there?
Do you like new houses?

Present simple statements
It's got two bedrooms.
They are small/large.

There + be
There is a garage.
There are three bedrooms.
Are there two bathrooms?

Possessives
my

expressions: not very
that's right.

Vocabulary

buy	living room
like	dining room
	bedroom
large	kitchen
small	bathroom
old	garden
new	garage
adj.: double	house
	flat

nouns: life, number, people, size, type.
determiners: all   a lot of

in England.

6 Ask and answer in pairs. (in Italy)
How many bedrooms are there in your house/flat? (bathrooms, living rooms...)
– There is/are _____.
Is it/are they large or small?
– It is _____/One is _____/Two are _____/ They are _____.

7 Listen to the tape. Mr Graves is talking about **B**. Is he right or wrong? There's 1 living room, the gdn is sml, 1 bdr. is lge + kitchen is 11 sq. mtrs.

8 Write about your house.
I live in a _____. There are _____ bedrooms. There is/isn't a _____. My living room is _____ and my kitchen is _____ sq. m.

7

Come to BRITAIN on holiday

Edinburgh

St Ives

Exeter

8

STAY IN A HOTEL

	Full board*	Half board	Bed & Breakfast	Bath/ Shower	Price category** A	B	C	D	E
Hotel David Edinburgh	√			√	√				
Hotel Portdown St Ives		√		√			√		
Devonia Hotel Exeter			√					√	
Queen Mary Hotel London		√						√	

STAY IN A PUB***

	Full board*	Half board	Bed & Breakfast	Bath/ Shower	Price category** A	B	C	D	E
The Half Moon			√					√	
The Swan		√		√			√		
The Old Manor House			√						√
The Stag			√						√

* Full board = room, breakfast, dinner and lunch
Half board = room, breakfast and dinner
Bed and breakfast = room, and breakfast

** Prices per person, per night
A = over £50 B = £35–50 C = £20–35
D = £12–£20 E = under £12

*** The pubs in the chart are all in the country, the hotels are all in towns.

Note: In the hotels and pubs:
Breakfast is from 7.30 to 9.30 am
Lunch is from 12.00 to 2.30 pm
Dinner is from 6.45 to 9.30 pm

STAY IN A HOLIDAY FLAT

	beds	cooker	fridge	washing machine	video	TV	radio	phone	price
Edinburgh	3	√	√	√		√		√	C
St Ives	5	√	√	√		√		√	B
Exeter	5	√	√				√	√	C
London	3	√	√		√	√		√	A

Prices per person, per week
A = over £50   B = between £30 and £50   C = under £30

London

1 Listen to the tape and look at the first two tables. Which hotel/pub is it?
H. Portdown.

2 You want to come to Britain on holiday.
Decide: the place (town/country)
the cost (A,B,C,D,E)
the type of hotel (full board/half board/bed and breakfast)
the type of room (with/without bath or shower)
Write down the information.

How much …?
It costs between £20 → £35 a night.

3 Now find a good hotel/pub, using your notes.
Ask about your partner's hotel.
Is there half board/full board at the ____?
– Yes, there is./No, there isn't.
Are there rooms with a bath at the ____?
– Yes, there are rooms with a bath at the ____.
How much does it cost at the ____?
– It costs over/under/between ____ and ____.
What time is breakfast at the ____?
– It's ____.

My husband and me.
For how many people?

* explain

4 Look at the third chart. Ask and answer in pairs.
Is there a ____ in the flat in London? – Yes, there is./No, there isn't.
How much does the flat in London cost? – It costs ____ per person.
How many beds are there in the flat in London? – There are ____.

5 Write the answers to these questions.
How many people are there in your family? – There are ____.
How much money have you got for your holiday flat? – We've got ____.
Do you want a washing machine in your holiday flat?
   (TV, video, radio, phone …)

Choose a holiday flat for your family.

6 Ask your partner the questions from Exercise 5, and write the answers.
Choose a holiday flat for him/her.

7 Two families are staying in holiday flats: the Schmidts, from Hamburg, and the Duponts, from Calais.
● There are three people in the German family. They are staying for two weeks. It costs £400. Where are they staying? *London.*
● There are five people in the French family. They are staying for three weeks. It costs £675. Where are they staying? *St. Ives.*

8 Listen to the tape and complete the chart.

Minchhampton Village	Rooms	Price	Telephone
The Elm			
Hotel Placide			
Singing Fiddle			

9 Complete the chart.   *verb. want*

write ans: In the country; A hotel; Yes; Full board.

Where do you want to stay?	_____
Do you want a hotel, flat or pub?	_____
Do you want a bath/shower in your room?	_____
Do you want price category A, B, C, D or E?	_____
Do you want bed and breakfast, half board or full board?	_____
How many people are there in your family?	_____

Sts. to ask quests. using "want".

Now give the information to your partner. He/she chooses a hotel/flat/pub for you. Write a short paragraph about it, like this: The Hotel Placide is in . .

Now you can:

talk about hotels and flats
talk about prices

KEY GRAMMAR
Question forms
How much does it cost?
Where do you want to stay?
Have you got a room?

Short forms
Yes, we have.
Yes, there is/are.
No, there isn't/aren't.

Present simple statements
It costs twenty pounds.
There is only one hotel.
There are rooms with a bath.

Prepositions
It costs over £5.
It costs under £10.
It costs between £5 and £10.
I want to stay for one night.
… a room with a bath.

Vocabulary
cost
have got
stay
want

flat
hotel
pub

bed and breakfast
full board
half board

country
town

8

Who works forty hours

Question uds: When? Why? How long? Because...

Pronouns apostrophe **Possessives** —'s *their our my your*

A lot of people work between 32 and 40 hours a week, and have three, four or five weeks' holiday a year. But this isn't always true. We talk to four people about their work and their holidays.

Ask: How many hours does Isabella work?

Where do Tom & Alex work?

9

Isabella works 70 hours a week. She works every day. Her holiday is only one week a year.

pt ast possessives

1 Listen to the tape. When is Isabella's holiday? *feb.*

Tom and Alex work in an oil refinery. They work six days a week. They work on Sunday. Their holiday this year is in August.

pt out possessives

Listen to the tape. When is their day off? *fri*

Fred Brown lives in England. He works 75 hours a week and has only one week's holiday a year. This year his holiday is in November. He has no days off in the week.

Listen to the tape. Where does he work? *On a farm*

Carlotta doesn't have a holiday. She works seven days a week.

Listen to the tape. <u>Why</u> doesn't Carlotta have a holiday?

Bcs she's got 8 children./ Bcs she wks very hard in the house.

a week?

then Ask →

2 Ask and answer in pairs.
Do you work hard in the house?
– Yes, I do./No, I don't.
How many days a week do you work?
When is your day off?
When is your holiday?

3 Look at the chart below. Read the passage on the right, fill in the missing numbers and work out the 'average' column.

Some statistics

In Europe the working week is quite good, and so is the working year. In the UK the average factory worker works forty hours a week and has four weeks' holiday a year. In West Germany the average working week is also forty hours, but the average holiday is six weeks. France has an average working week of thirty-nine hours, with five weeks' holiday. Switzerland has a long working week – forty-three hours – and average holidays of four weeks a year.

	UK	USA	W. Germany	France	Japan	Switzerland	Hong Kong	Average
*hours per week	40	40	40	39	40	48	48	42 (295÷7)
holidays per year (weeks)	4 wks	4½	6 wks	5 wks	4	4	1½	3.3 (24÷7=)

*Statistics are for a factory worker.

4 Ask and answer questions about the statistics in pairs, like this:
How long is the working week in France?
How long is a worker's holiday in Japan?

5 Group survey
In groups of four, complete the table below. Ask and answer the questions.

	Person A	Person B	Person C	Person D
Do you have a job outside your house?				
Do you work in the house?				
How many hours a week do you work in your job? in your house?				
When is your holiday?				
How long is your holiday?				
When are your days off?				

6 Write a summary.
In this group ____ people have got work outside the house. The group ____ an average of ____ hours in a job and an average of ____ hours in ____. ____ have got a holiday this year. The average number of weeks' holiday is ____.

SUMMARY

Now you can:

talk about holidays, when they are and how long they are

KEY GRAMMAR
Question forms
When is your day off?
Why don't you have a holiday?
How long is the working week?

Present simple statements
I have a holiday in February.
I've got eight children.
She doesn't have a holiday.

Connectors
She doesn't have a holiday because she's got eight children.

Possessives
Isabella's
their
my
your
his
her

Vocabulary
average
day off
holiday
week
year

Months
January
February
March
April
May
June
July
August
September
October
November
December

Days
Sunday
Monday
Tuesday
Wednesday
Thursday
Friday
Saturday

9

1 Introducing oneself
I'm John Robins. How do you do?
– I'm Lise Braun. How do you do?

2 Greeting
Hello, Mary. How are you?
– Fine thanks. How are you?
Very well, thanks.

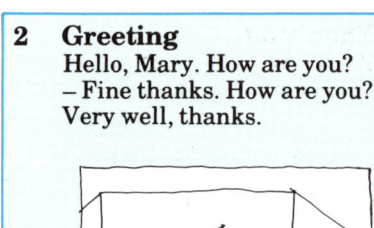

3 Introducing
I'd like you to meet my sister, Jane.
– Hello, Jane. Nice to meet you.

4 Introducing
Paula, this is my brother, Bob.
– Hello, Bob. Pleased to meet you.

5 Apologising
Hello, everyone. I'm sorry I'm late.
– That's all right.

6 Apologising
Hello, Mary. I'm sorry I'm late. Is that our train?
– Yes, but it doesn't matter. How are you?

10

Odile is French but she lives in London. Her cartoons are famous in France. Here she looks at the British.

1 Listen to the tape and look at the cartoons. Act out the situations with a partner.

2 Do you say the right things? Complete the quiz below.

1 You're greeting a friend. What do you say?
2 You're introducing a friend. What do you say? (Two things.)
3 A friend is introducing his/her sister. What do you say? (Two things.)
4 You're late. Apologise.
5 A friend is apologising. What do you say?
6 You want to leave. What do you say?
7 A friend gives you a gift. What do you say?
8 You're introducing yourself. What do you say?

Fill in the gaps. Then work out your score.

	right	wrong
Greeting _____		
Introducing a) _____		
b) _____		
Answering an introduction a) _____		
b) _____		
Apologising _____		
Answering an apology _____		
Leaving _____		
Thanking _____		
Introducing yourself _____		
Your score =		Total = 10

7 Apologising
I am sorry!
– It doesn't matter.

8 Thanking
Thank you very much.
– Don't mention it.

9 Leaving
I must go, Paula. Thank you very much.
– It was nice to see you, John.

10 Leaving
I have to go now. Goodbye, father.
– Goodbye, Richard.

3 Do you say the right things? Speak together in pairs.

How do you do?

Hello, how are you?

I'd like you to meet, Bob.
He's my brother.

Mary, this is my sister, Jane.

I'm sorry I'm late.

I am sorry!

Thank you very much.

I must go. Thank you very much.

I have to go now.

4 Listen to the situations on the tape. Some of the replies are wrong. Which ones? Correct them and write them down.

5 Act out the correct situations with your partner.

6 Game
Write a situation from the cartoons (eg greeting, apologising) on a piece of paper. Put all the pieces of paper together. One person takes a piece of paper and reads the word. He/she then chooses two/three people to act out the situation.

SUMMARY

Now you can:

introduce yourself
greet people
introduce others
apologise
thank
say goodbye

Vocabulary
have to
meet
must
sorry
friend

Guinness, garlic and ginseng:

All of these people are 100 years old, or more.

1 Read the information about these people, then complete the tables.

Flory

Children:

Grandchildren:

Daughter's name:

Valerie

Age:

Lives alone?

Children:

Nikolai

Age:

Lives alone?

Country:

Tan

Age:

Children:

Age of brother:

Age of sister:

2 Ask and answer in pairs.
How old is Flory?
– She's 101.
How many sons has she got?
(daughters, children, brothers . . .)
– She's got ____.
How old is Flory's daughter? (sister, son, wife, mother . . .)
– She's ____.

Flory O'Grady lives in Ireland. She is 101 years old. She's got six sons, four daughters and 45 grandchildren. Flory's husband is dead. She lives with her daughter, Mary. Mary is 77.

Valerie is 100. She lives in Bulgaria. She's got twelve children. She always sleeps twelve hours a night and eats a lot of yoghurt. Valerie's husband is dead too.

3 Listen to the tape and take notes.

His/her name is ____.

He/she is ____ years old.

He/she's got ____ children.

He/she always ____.

He/she never ____.

	Person 1	Person 2

4 Now ask and answer in pairs.
What's his/her name?
How old is he/she?
How many children has he/she got?
What does he/she always/never do?

5 These four people are very old. Use *always* and *never* and write sentences like this:
Flory never drinks tea.

Now write sentences about yourself.
What do you always/never drink?
What do you always/never eat?

6 Find out about your partner's family. Use these questions:
How old are you?
– I am ____.
How old are your parents?
– My mother/father is ____.
Have you got any brothers or sisters?
– Yes, I have./No, I haven't.
How many brothers/sisters have you got?
– I've got ____.
How old is he/she? (are they?)
– He/she is ____. (They are ____.)

how to live to be 100

SUMMARY

Now you can:

say how old you are
talk about your family

KEY GRAMMAR
Question forms
How old are you?
Have you got any brothers?
How many sisters have you got?

Present simple statements
He always eats garlic.
He never eats any sugar.
He's 45 years old.
She's got eleven children.

Possessive + 's
Flory's husband is dead.

Determiners
He never eats any sugar.
I always have some fruit for
    breakfast.

Vocabulary

mother	father
wife	husband
daughter	son
sister	brother
parents	
grandmother/father	

alive
dead

drink
eat

Nikolai is 105. He lives in
Georgia, USSR. People in Georgia
eat a lot of garlic. His wife is also
alive. She is 103.

Tan is 103 years old. He's got
seventeen children. His brother
and sister are both still alive. His
brother is 98 and his sister is 94.
He always eats ginseng and never
eats any sugar.

7 Group survey: family portraits
In groups of four ask and answer the
questions to complete this table,
for example:

*How many of your grandparents are
alive?*
– Three (two . . .) are alive.
Write the number in the table.

	Person A	Person B	Person C	Person D
Grandparents: How many of your grandparents are alive? How old is/are your grandmother(s)? How old is/are your grandfather(s)?				
Brothers/sisters: How many brothers have you got? How old are they? How many sisters have you got? How old are they?				
Children: Have you got any children? How many children have you got? Have you got any daughters? How many? How old are they? Have you got any sons? How many? How old are they?				

Average number of children per
family in this group:
Total number of sons:
Total number of daughters:
Total number of brothers:
Total number of sisters:
Number of grandparents alive in
this group:
Average age of grandparents in this
group:

8 Write a summary of your group.
Start like this:
In our group there are _____ children,
_____ sons and _____ daughters. There
are _____ brothers . . .

11

REVISION

Dear Carrie

When the English meet someone for the first time, what do they say?
Yours sincerely Brigitte

Dear Brigitte
Thank you for your letter. When people meet for the first time they say 'How do you do?' The answer is 'How do you do?' Carrie

Dear Carrie
What do you say in English when you are late? Do you say 'I'm sorry I'm late?'
Yours sincerely Monique

1 Letter-writing

Reply to Monique's letter.
Then write a letter to Carrie.
Ask how to introduce a friend to another person.

2 Match the cartoon with the phrase.
1 Hello, how are you?
2 I'm sorry I'm late.
3 I must go now.
Thank you very much.
4 Oh, I am sorry.
5 I'm John Tunnis.

A

B

C

5 Complete the weekly calendar:

JUNE	
Monday 15th	———— 19th
———— 16th	———— 20th
———— 17th	———— 21st
———— 18th	

6 Write the names of the months in the correct column.

28/29 days	30 days	31 days

7 Here are some verbs from units 7–11. What are they?

MO_E W_NT ST_Y WR_T_
ME_N CO_T LI_TEN T_LK

Now make sentences, using these verbs:
1 I ____ to speak English.
2 He ____ good books.
3 She is ____ to music.
4 I am ____ in Montmartre at the moment.
5 What does this word ____ ?

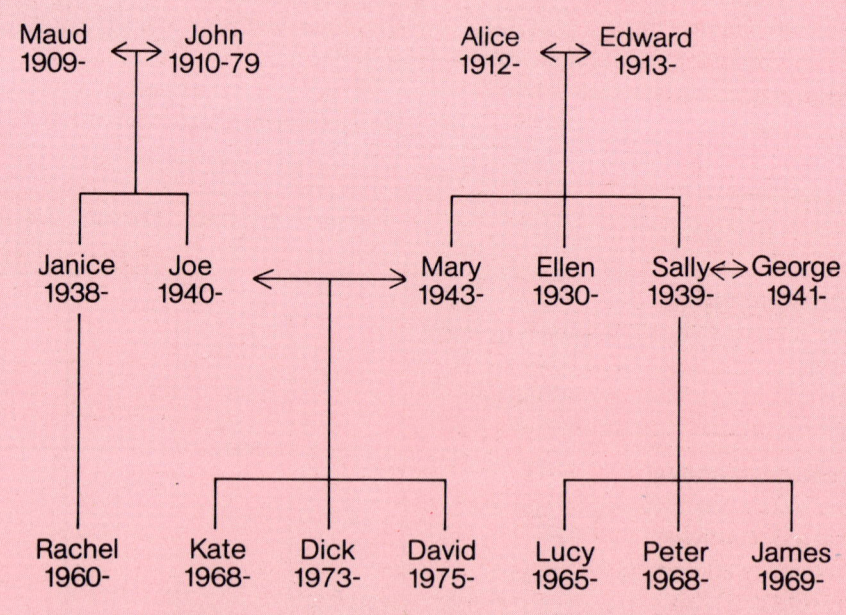

8 Ask your partner questions like the ones below.
Who is ____'s son?
How many brothers has ____ got?
How old is ____ ?
(Use *mother/father/son/daughter/sister/brother/ grandmother/grandfather/aunt/uncle/cousin/ grandchildren*)

12

D

E

3 Ask and answer questions.

How many | *people/rooms/animals/adults/ windows/televisions/doors/ bedrooms* | *are there in your house?*

– There are ___ in my house.

4 Write your own measurements for the rooms in this flat:

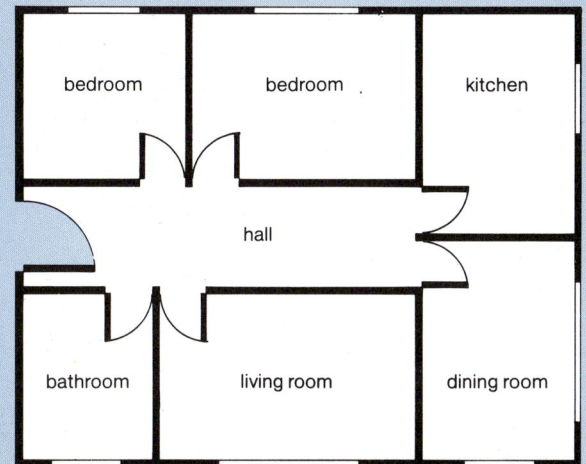

Now ask your partner questions, like this:

How large is your kitchen/ dining room/flat?

12

QUIZ

9 Match the words and numbers.

| Days in a week |
| Months in a year |
| Minutes in an hour |
| Days in a year |
| Days in February |
| Days in October |
| Hours in a week |
| Seconds in an hour |

60		3600
	365	
		31
12	28	
	168
7	

POTATOES 1 KILO 39P

MILK 4 LITRES £1.60

APPLES 2 KILOS £1.95

BEEF 2 KILOS £5.68

TOMATOES 2 KILOS £2.10

BREAD 48P

FISH 1½ KILOS £3.25

10 Look at the list and ask questions, like this: *How much does a litre of milk cost?*

DIET & EXERCISE
DO YOU EAT THE RIGHT FOOD?

A lot of people never exercise. They often eat the wrong food as well. These people become unhealthy. Linda Gaven talks to three people about their health: Paula, a dancer; Peter, a jockey and John, an actor. All of them are careful about their food and exercise a lot.

Paula is a dancer and she exercises a lot. She runs about five kilometres every day, and at the weekend she does aerobics.

1 Listen to the tape and complete the diet table for Paula. What else does Paula eat and what does she drink?

2 Ask and answer in pairs.
Does Paula eat/drink any _____ ?
– Yes, she does./No, she doesn't.

3 Paula has some fruit for breakfast. Now ask and answer in pairs.
What do you have for breakfast?
(lunch, dinner)
– I have _____./I always have _____.

Peter is thirty-two. He is very healthy. He likes swimming and running. He doesn't drink any alcohol and he never smokes.

4 Listen to the tape and complete the diet table for Peter.

5 Ask and answer in pairs.
What do you drink?
– I always/never drink _____ .
What do you eat a lot of?
– I eat a lot of _____ .
What do you eat every morning?
– Every morning I eat _____ .
What don't you eat?
– I don't eat any _____/I never eat any _____ .

6 Look at these sentences from the tape:

Linda Peter, how often do you exercise?

Peter I swim and run every day.

Ask people in the class and fill in the table below.
How often do you exercise?

never	every day	every week

13

Diet table	Paula	Peter	John	Your partner
meat				
fish				
eggs				
vegetables				
fruit				
milk/cheese				
sugar				
coffee/tea				
alcohol				
brown bread/cereal				

13

7 John never eats any meat. He is a vegetarian. He is an actor and he likes yoga. What does he eat? Talk to your partner and complete the table for John.

8 Complete the table for your partner. Ask and answer in pairs.
Do you eat/drink any _____ ?
– Yes, I do./No, I don't.

9 Agree or disagree with the statements below, like this:
A lot of meat is good for you.
– I agree./Yes, it is.
– No, it isn't, it's bad for you.

A lot of eggs are bad for you.
A lot of vegetables are bad for you.
A lot of sugar is good for you.
A lot of coffee is bad for you.
A lot of alcohol is bad for you.
A lot of cereal is good for you.

10 Write about your diet:
I always eat _____, but I never eat _____. I often eat _____ ; it's _____ for you. For breakfast I eat _____, for lunch _____ and for dinner _____. I drink a lot of _____ but I never drink any _____.

Write about exercise (from Exercise 6):
I exercise every _____. In my class _____ people never _____, _____ people exercise _____ and _____ exercise _____.

DIET & EXERCISE
ARE YOU AVERAGE?

These people are not average. They are taller or shorter, heavier or thinner than other people. Mario is very tall, in fact he's 1.95 m tall, but Ariane is very short; she's only 1.42 m tall.

Some people are very fat, some are very thin. Look at Josef, he's fat. He weighs about 90 kg but he's only 1.60 m tall. He's too fat. Joanna's very thin; she weighs only 45 kg, but she's also quite tall.

1 Who is A?

A =

B =

C =

D =

2 Who is it?
Talk about the pictures. Do not name the person.
Say: *He/she is too/quite/very heavy.*
(thin, tall, short, fat)
Other people ask and answer.
Is it _____?
– No, it isn't./Yes, it is.

3 Ask and answer in pairs.
How tall are you?
– I'm _____ m tall.
How heavy are you?
– I'm about _____ kg.

4 Game
Talk about someone in the class, in your pairs. Do not name the person.
Say: *He/she is taller than I am.*
(shorter, heavier, thinner, fatter)
Is it _____?
– No, it isn't./Yes, it is.

A   B   C   D

5 Look at the table, listen to the tape and fill in the gaps.

Height:	1.45 m	1.5 m	1.55 m	1.6 m	1.65 m	1.7 m	1.75 m	1.8 m	1.85 m	1.9 m
Men			56 kg	59k	62 kg	66 kg	69.5 kg	75½k	77.5 kg	82 kg
Women	47 kg	50kg	52.5 kg	56 kg	60kg	63.5 kg	67 kg	71 kg		

The weights are for people with medium build.
Do you weigh more or less than the average?

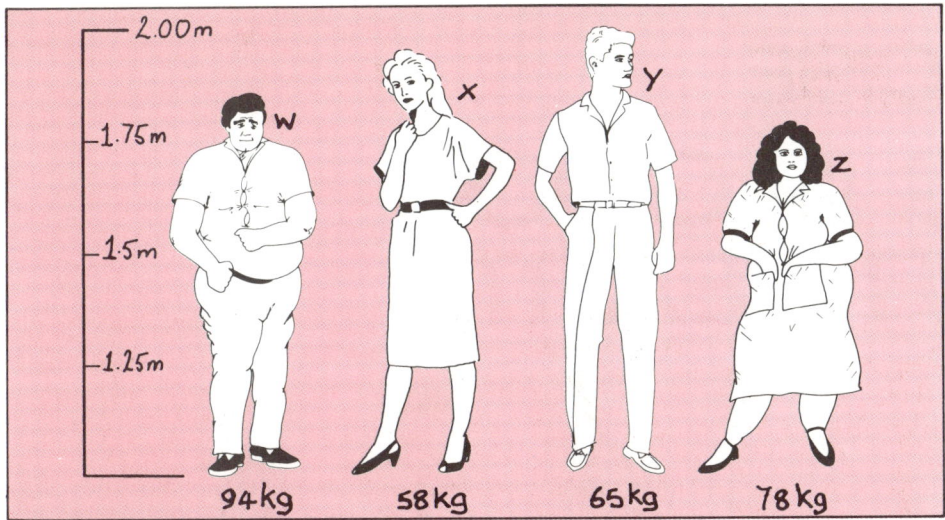

94 kg   58 kg   65 kg   78 kg

6   Look at the people above.
Ask and answer.
How tall is W? (X,Y,Z)
How heavy is W? (X,Y,Z)
Does W weigh more or less than the average? (X,Y,Z)
Is W a policeman?
– No, he's too short.
Is Y a jockey?
– No, ____

7   Make a form like the one on the right. Fill it in for yourself. Give all the forms to your teacher. Your teacher will give you a different form. Write sentences about the person and read them out, but do not read out the name.
He/she is ____ old, he/she is ____ tall, he/she weighs ____ kg. Who is it?

8   Group survey
Ask and answer in groups of four.

Job Requirements

Policeman	more than 1.72 m
Policewoman	more than 1.67 m
Air hostess	more than 1.57 m
	less than 56 kg
Jockey	less than 63 kg
Model	more than 1.65 m

Name _____

Male/female _____

Age _____

Height _____

Weight _____

14

Do you watch television?

per week	1	2	3	4
one evening				
two evenings				
three evenings				
four evenings				
more				

Do you read books?

per month	1	2	3	4
one				
two				
five				
ten				
more				

Do you eat in restaurants?

per month	1	2	3	4
one meal				
two meals				
three meals				
five meals				
more				

Use these questions:
How often do you watch television in a week?
How many books do you read in a month?
How many meals do you eat in restaurants in a month?
What's your group average?
Is it more or less than the average for other groups?

DIET & EXERCISE
JOGGING IS GOOD FOR YOUR HEART

What sports do they do?

	Jogging	73 people	A lot
	Swimming	35 people	Quite a lot
	Aerobics	10 people	A few/not many
	Yoga	5 people	Very few
	Tennis	30 people	Quite a lot
	Climbing	2 people	Very few
	Cycling	12 people	A few/not many
Other sports		18 people	Quite a few

These tables come from a survey of 100 people. They all do sports. Some do a lot of sports, but some do only a few. Look at the table, more than 50 per cent do only one sport. A lot of people jog. Quite a lot of people swim. Not many people do aerobics and very few people climb.

How many sports do they do?	
1 sport	52%
2 sports	25%
3 sports	17%
4 sports	4%
5 or more	2%
	100%

SUMMARY

Now you can :

say why you like something
talk about sports
use numbers

KEY GRAMMAR
Question forms
How many sports do you do?
Why does he like it?
How many people swim?
What is it good for?

Present simple statements
I don't do any sports.
He likes swimming because . . .
Some sports are expensive, some
   are cheap.
Jogging is good for your heart.

Number
very few
a few
not many
quite a lot
a lot

Vocabulary

climb	relaxing
cycle	fun
do { aerobics, yoga, sport }	arms
	legs
jog	back
lose	heart
play tennis	breathing
expensive	
cheap	
exciting	

1 Class survey
Do a survey of the class in groups.
Ask these questions:
How many people don't do any sports?
How many people do one sport?
How many people do two sports?
   (three, four . . .)

number of sports	number of people
0	
1	
2	
3	
4	
5	
more	

2 Ask and answer in groups.
How many people swim?

sport	people
swim	
jog	
do aerobics	
do yoga	
play tennis	
climb	
cycle	
do other sports	
don't do any sports	

3 Now write a summary of your group.
In this group not many people ____ . A lot of people ____ . More than ____ per cent ____ . Quite a lot of people ____ but very few ____ . Nobody ____ .

People do sports for different reasons. Some sports are expensive and some are cheap. Some are exciting and some are relaxing. Swimming is good for your arms and so is tennis. Cycling is good for your legs. Jogging is good for losing weight and for your heart.

4 Listen to the tape and complete the table.
The interview is with Heinrich.
He does a lot of sports.

What is it good for?
   Write the letter (ABCDEF) only.
Why does he like it?
   Write the number (1234) only.

	What is it good for?	Why does he like it?
swimming		
tennis		
cycling		
yoga		
jogging		

A your back
B your legs
C your heart
D losing weight
E breathing
F your arms

1 it's not expensive
2 it's relaxing
3 it's fun
4 it's exciting

5 Now write about Heinrich.
Heinrich likes ____ because it's good for ____ and because ____ . He also likes ____ . . .

6 Work with a partner. Write down two or more sports you like.
Interview each other, like this:

A How many sports do you do?
B ____ .
A And what are they?
B ____ and ____ .
A Why do you like ____ ?
B Because it's ____ .
A You also do ____ ?
B Yes, it's ____ and it's ____ .

7 Write about the sports you and your partner like.
I like ____ because it's ____ and it's ____ . I also like ____ because ____ . My partner likes ____ . . .

15

GETTING THERE

Bina is a small Thai town. There are only about a hundred cars in the town, but every Wednesday there is a market; lots of people come to buy and sell different things and there is always a traffic jam. People come in many different ways. Some come by bus. Some come by train. The town is on a river and a lot of people come by boat. A lot of other people come on foot.

16

This boy comes on foot. It's easy because he lives only a few hundred metres away. He wants to buy a bicycle but he hasn't got any money.

This young woman and her child come by bus. It's not very safe and it's not very comfortable, but it's cheap.

This man comes by bicycle. He doesn't like buses or trains. He's never been on a train; they are too modern. Bicycles are slow and safe.

Somsak comes by motorbike. It's very dangerous and also very dirty. He likes it because it's fast.

Apa comes by train. She hasn't got a car and she's never been on a motorbike because they're dangerous. She sells food in her shop at the market.

This young girl comes by boat. She likes the boat because it's cheap and easy. She lives near the river.

1 Ask and answer in pairs.
How does the young boy go to Bina?
(young woman, man, Somsak, Apa, young girl)
– He/she goes ____ .
Why does/doesn't ____ like ____ ?
– He/she likes/doesn't like ____ because ____ .

2 Ask and answer in pairs.
Has the man ever been on a ____ ?
– No, he's never been on a ____ .
Has Apa ____ ?
– No, ____ .
Have you ever been on a plane?
(boat, hovercraft, motorbike, bicycle . . .)
– Yes, I have./No, I haven't.

3 Listen to the tape and fill in the gaps.
It's Saturday morning in Bina, and on Saturdays hundreds of people come into the town to ____ . I've got a car here but there aren't many cars in the town. People come ____ . I've never been on a riverboat. They're ____ and ____ . The buses are ____ . ____ on a bus here in Thailand – they're not very ____ .

4 Talk to your partner and take notes.
Ask these questions:
How do you come to class?
Why do you come by/on ____ ?
How do you go shopping?
Where do you buy your shopping?

Notes
____ comes to class by/on ____ because ____ .
____ goes shopping ____ at ____ .

5 Talk to your partner, like this:
I like/don't like buses (trains, boats, planes, bicycles, motorbikes . . .)
– Why?
Because they're ____ .

6 Now write about yourself. Answer the questions above.

7 Listen to the tape and complete the information in the table below.

	Mario	**Paolo**	**Teresa**
likes			
because			
doesn't like	planes		
because	they're dangerous		

8 Work in pairs. Ask and answer questions, using these words:

cheap	slow	clean	safe	comfortable
expensive	fast	dirty	dangerous	uncomfortable

Do you like trains? (buses, bicycles, planes, cars . . .)
– Yes, I do, because ____ ./No, I don't, because ____ .

9 Now tell the class about your partner.
____ likes trains because ____ , but he/she doesn't like ____ because ____ .

16

SUMMARY

Now you can:

talk about travel
say how often you do things

KEY GRAMMAR
Question forms
How does he go to Bina?
Why don't you like trains?
Has he ever been on a plane?

Short forms
Yes, he has./No, he hasn't.

Present simple statements
He goes by bicycle/on foot.
I don't like buses because they're slow.

Present perfect statements
He's never been on a plane.

Prepositions
by boat/bus/train
on foot

Vocabulary
buy
go
sell

bicycle
boat
bus
car
motorbike
plane
train

clean
dirty
comfortable
uncomfortable
safe
dangerous

slow
fast

boy
girl
man
woman
young

Which car?

Which car is right for you? Of course, cost is important, but there are other questions. How big is your family? How fast do you drive? Do you drive long distances or short distances? Does a heavier car use more petrol?

Citroen Familiale

car	seats (larger/ smaller)	top speed (faster/ slower)	weight (approx) (heavier/ lighter)	price (cheaper/ more expensive)
Luxury	7	188 kph	1470 kg	*****
Family saloon	4/5	180 kph	1175 kg	**
Hatchback	4	150 kph	800 kg	*
Estate	5	160 kph	1300 kg	***
Sports	2	215 kph	1185 kg	****
Four-wheel drive	5	150 kph	1930 kg	****

* cheap   *** expensive

This table gives some facts about six types of car.

Is the Citroen the car for you? It's larger than a family saloon but faster than a four-wheel drive. It's heavier than an estate car, and more expensive.
– It's a luxury car.
What about the Metro? It's smaller than an estate car, lighter than a family car, and cheaper than both.
– It's a hatchback.

1   Listen to the tape and answer the questions.
Which type is Car A?/Which type is Car B?

2   Ask and answer in pairs.
Which car is larger than a ____?
  (faster, heavier, more expensive)
– The ____ is larger than a ____.
Which car is smaller than a ____?
  (slower, lighter, cheaper)
– The ____ is smaller than a ____.

3   Guess the car. Give two facts about a car.
Your partner guesses which car.
It's faster than a ____.
It's more expensive than a ____.
– Is it a ____?
Yes, it is./No, it isn't.

4   Listen to the tape and fill in the gaps.
A   Oh, look at that sports car.
B   It's going too fast.
A   ____ in a sports car?
B   No, ____ in a car like that.
A   It's very safe.
B   Yes, but it's also very fast. ____ in a sports car and I don't want to go in one.
A   Well, in my country people drive very fast. ____ to Germany?
B   No. ____ south of Dover.

Ford Sierra

Austin Metro

17

5 Ask and answer in pairs.
Have you ever been in a sports car?
(luxury car, four-wheel drive car ...)
– *Yes, I have./No, I haven't.*
Have you ever been to Rome?
(London, Athens, Frankfurt, Hong Kong ...)
– *Yes, I have./No, I haven't.*

6 Write down the name and year of a car and complete the table below.
Then ask your partner about his/her car.
How old is your car?
How much does it weigh?
How many seats has it got?
Which type is it?
Is it a ____?

	A	B
Age		
Weight		
Seats		
Type		
Name		

7 Now write about your partner's car, like this:
Peter's car is older than my car. It's got more seats but my car weighs more. His car is a ____ and my car is a ____.

Range Rover

Peugeot 505

Porsche 944

17

8 Listen to the tape. The young woman wants to buy a car. What does she want?

9 Roleplay
Work in pairs. **A** decides on a car. Listen to the tape and make a dialogue.
A Good morning. I want to buy a new car.
B What type ____?
A Well, I've got ____, and I ____.
B Do you drive a lot?
A ____, and I ____. Really, I want a ____.
B Well, I've got just the car for you. It's fantastic. It's a ____, it's ____ and ____ than ____, and it ____.

SUMMARY

Now you can:

talk and write about cars

KEY GRAMMAR
Question forms
Which car is right for you?
Which type is it?
How much does it weigh?
How many seats has it got?
Which car is larger than a hatchback?
Have you ever been to Rome?
Have you ever been in a sports car?

Making comparisons
It's larger than a hatchback.

Present perfect statements
I've never been to Rio de Janeiro.

Present simple statements
I've got just the car for you.
It's a luxury car.
It weighs more.

Vocabulary

drive	family saloon
fast	four wheel drive
(adjective/adverb)	hatchback
	luxury car
estate	sports car

REVISION

Dear Carrie

I am writing about my diet. I am very happy because I now weigh a lot less.
This is my diet for today:

Breakfast: one egg
              one grapefruit
              tea

Lunch: salad (lettuce, tomatoes, cucumber)
              one piece of toast

Dinner: steak
              peas
              carrots

There is no alcohol and very little salt in my diet. Every day I have a small lunch. Some days I have fruit juice in the morning with my egg. In the evening I have fish, turkey, chicken or beef. I eat quite a lot, but I am losing weight.
With best wishes,

Carole

Dear Carole
Some diets are good and some are bad. Yours is a good one and you look much thinner.

Carrie

1 Letter-writing

Write a letter to Carrie and tell her your diet for today.

2 Match the stamp to the country

Now ask and answer questions.
Have you ever been to _____?
Where else have you been in/outside Europe?

India Poland USA UK France Austria Turkey Spain New Zealand

3 Ask and answer in pairs.

Have you got any brothers?
*(sisters/animals/English friends/
foreign books/modern furniture)*
– { *Yes, I've got some/one/a _____.*
   No, I haven't got any.

4 Look at the table.

Ask and answer in pairs.
Which person is heavier?
– A is heavier.
Which car is faster?
– B is faster.

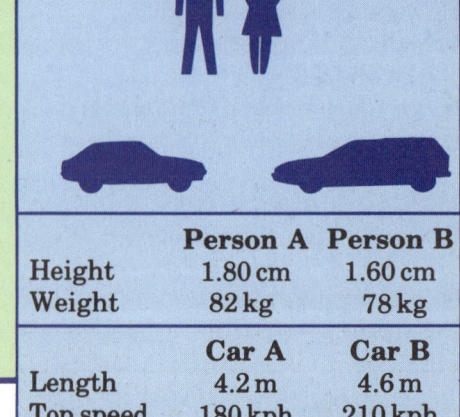

	Person A	Person B
Height	1.80 cm	1.60 cm
Weight	82 kg	78 kg
	Car A	**Car B**
Length	4.2 m	4.6 m
Top speed	180 kph	210 kph

5 Write sentences, like this:

A is	smaller larger more expensive cheaper	than B.
	as _____	as B.

6 Look at this table.
Make sentences, using the words below:
Few/not many/a lot of/quite a few/some/no/not any

Eg *There aren't many triangles in Column A.*

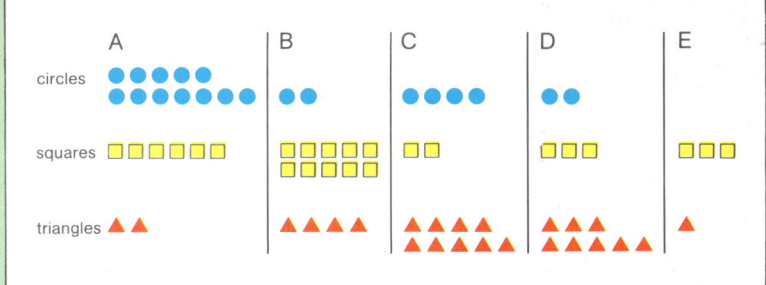

	A	B	C	D	E
circles	•••• / •••••	••	••••	••	
squares	□□□□□	□□□□□ / □□□□□	□□	□□□	□□□
triangles	▲▲	▲▲▲▲	▲▲▲▲ / ▲▲▲▲▲	▲▲▲ / ▲▲▲▲	▲

8 Here are some verbs from Units 13–17. What are they?

E_T   E_ERC_SE   L__K AT

DR__K   PL_Y   DR_VE

C_ME   B_COME   R_N

U_E   T_LL   LOV_

SW_M   CLI_B   A_K

9 Complete these sentences.
You _____ fruit.
You _____ a car.
You _____ water.
You _____ a letter.
You _____ tennis.
You _____ clothes.
You _____ food at a shop.

10 Crossword
Complete this crossword with words from Units 13–17.

1			2		3
4		5			
				6	

DOWN
1 I've got _____ water.
2 I come to work _____ my car.
3 I like jogging, because it's good for my _____.
5 I haven't got _____ money.

ACROSS
4 I like an _____ in the morning.
6 He comes by bus _____ on foot.

7 Look at the pictures.
Ask and answer in pairs.
How do you say _____ in English?

Now talk about the pictures, like this:
Every week I eat some _____, but I don't have any _____. What do you eat?

less waiting in line   earlier flights, later flights

19   Come on board and see the

1   Listen to the tape. It is an advertisement for TOA airlines. Complete the table below.

Compare before you fly.

Compare TOA with two other international airlines. (All flights are from London.)

	TOA	ACB	WA
Number of destinations		6	7
Number of flights per day		28	24
Number of early flights (before 8 am)	3	1	—
Number of morning flights (8–12.00 am)		11	8
Number of afternoon flights (12.00–6 pm)		8	12
Number of late flights (6.00–10.00 pm)		7	4
Number of night flights (after 10.00 pm)	2	1	—
Number of check-in counters		2	3
Number of seats across in cabin		6	7 or 8
Leg room per passenger		75 cm	70 cm

2   Complete these sentences with *more, fewer* or *less*.
1   ACB's got <u>fewer</u> destinations than WA.
2   ACB's got ____ leg room than WA.
3   WA's got ____ late flights than ACB.
4   WA ____ fewer ____ than ACB.
5   ACB ____ more ____ than WA.
6   ACB ____ morning flights ____ WA.

3   Write four more sentences about ACB and WA.

4   Look at the information for ACB and WA. Ask and answer in pairs.
Which airline's got more ____?
– ACB has./WA has. It's got more ____ than ____.

5   Say why you think TOA is better than ACB and WA. Write three sentences, like this:
ACB is good, but TOA is better because it has more ____ .

6   Listen to the tape and complete the menu.

7   Ask and answer in pairs.
What would you like to eat?
– I'd like fruit juice, chicken with fried rice, apple pie, and a lager, please.

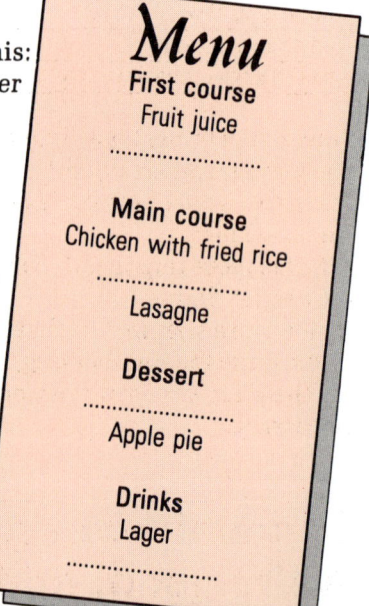

Menu
First course
Fruit juice
....

Main course
Chicken with fried rice
....
Lasagne
....

Dessert
....
Apple pie
....

Drinks
Lager
....

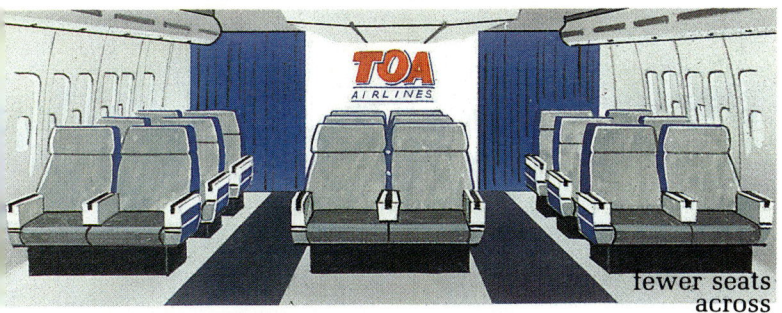

fewer seats across

more leg room

better menus

TOA 141	NEW YORK	13·00
TOA 142	MADRID	13·20
TOA 144	PARIS	14·15
TOA 147	NEW YORK	15·20
TOA 150	MILAN	16·00

afternoon flights to New York

difference!

8   What is important about an airline?
Look at the table, and fill it in about yourself with the numbers 1 (more important) to 6 (less important).

	you	tape	your partner
better menus			
cheaper flights			
more leg room			
fewer seats across			
better flight service			
more check-in counters			

Now listen to the tape. Every time the interviewer asks the young woman a question, write a star (*) next to the thing the woman thinks is more important in the chart.
For example:
What is more important, better menus or cheaper flights?
– Cheaper flights.
You write a star next to cheaper flights.
Then write the numbers, eg 5 stars = 1, 4 stars = 2 etc.
Do the same with your partner. Listen to the tape again if necessary.

9   Complete these words, and then make sentences, like this:
c_nc_ll_tions
cancellations
TOA has fewer cancellations than ACB.
fl_g_ts
s__ts _cross
l_g ro_m per passenger
ch_ck-_n c__nters

Some airlines go from bad to worse.
We're good, and we're getting better and better.

Tom was a cook.
He's now a postman.

Joe was an accountant.
He's now unemployed.

20

OUT OF WORK

These people all worked in John Dobson's Ltd, a clothes factory. It closed five years ago and now the factory is empty. There were 350 people in Dobson's Ltd. There were factory workers and accountants, secretaries and managers. There were fifteen drivers and six cooks. What happened to them when the factory closed? Some were lucky; they're working now, but more than a hundred, like Joe, are still unemployed.

Brian was a driver.
He's now self-employed.
He's got his own shop.

Joan was a manager.
She's now retired.

Roger was a factory worker.
He now works in a bank.

Gloria was a secretary.
She's now a teacher.

1 Ask and answer in pairs.
What was Joan? (Tom, Brian, Roger, Gloria, Joe)
– She was ____.
What does she do now?
– She's ____.

2 Look at the text.
Find the past tense of these verbs.

Irregular   is   are
Regular   happen   close   work

3 Listen to the tape and answer the questions.
1 Roger lost his job in the factory.
What happened next?   i) ____
                         ii) ____
                         iii) ____
What does he do now?   He still ____.
2 Joan lost her job in the factory.
What happened next?   ____
What does she do now?   ____

4 Ask and answer in pairs.
What did you do five years ago?
– I worked in a ____.
– I was (a/an) ____.
What do you do now?
– I (still) work in a ____.
– I'm (still) (a/an) ____.

5 Now change partners and ask again.

6 Group survey

How many people have changed jobs in the last five years? Work in groups of four. Complete the table for your group. Ask and answer the questions.

2 What did you do then?
Name _____
Name _____
Name _____
Name _____

3 What do you do now?
Name _____
Name _____
Name _____
Name _____

1 Have you changed your job in the last five years?

Name	Yes	No
Name _____		
Name _____		
Name _____		
Name _____		

I worked in a/an				I was a		I was	
factory	office	school	other	student	housewife	unemployed	retired

I work in a/an				I am a		I am	
factory	office	school	other	student	housewife	unemployed	retired

7 Write about your survey
Five years ago I ____. No, I'm ____. *(Name)* was ____. Now he ____.
(Name) was ____ but now she ____, and *(Name)* was ____ but now he ____.

20

SUMMARY

Now you can :

talk about your job now
talk about your job in the past

KEY GRAMMAR
Question forms
What was Joan?
What happened five years ago?
What happened next?
What do you do now?
Have you changed your job in the last five years?

Present simple statements
I'm unemployed.
I'm still an accountant.

Past simple statements
She was a manager.
She lost her job.
He worked in a factory.
There were 350 people.

Present perfect short forms
Yes, I have./No, I haven't.

Vocabulary
change (changed)   secretary
close (closed)   student
happen (happened)   teacher
lose (lost)
                        factory
accountant   retired
cook   self-employed
driver   unemployed
housewife
manager
postman

MURDER AT THE HOTEL!

Have you ever read a book by Agatha Christie? She was a writer, a detective story writer. Do you like detective stories? In Britain some people go on 'Murder Weekends' at hotels. Someone finds a dead body and the hotel guests are the detectives: they talk to people, find clues and in the end they find the murderer! There was a murder last weekend at the Downs Hotel. Mr Price, a detective, talked to these people:

Pierre is a cook. He comes from Paris. He usually works in the kitchen.

4   Pierre is a cook. Consuela is a maid. What do you do?
Say: *I am a _____ (professore, medico, Anwalt, estudiante . . .)*
Ask your teacher: *How do you say it in English?*
                              How do you spell it?

Write: *I am a _____ .*
Now ask around the class:
I'm a/an _____ . What do you do?

5   Class survey
Ask questions of the class:
Who is a doctor? Who is a student?
Make a list: *doctors – 1*
                      students – 3
                      secretaries – 5
Now write about the people in your class.

Consuela found the dead body Sunday morning at ten o'clock in a hotel bedroom. She didn't find any clues. The dead man was a policeman. Mr Price wants to find the murderer. It's now Sunday afternoon and he is talking to the people in the hotel.

1   Ask and answer questions about these people:
Who works in the kitchen? (dining room, lobby, office, bedrooms)
– Pierre does.
Who comes from France? (Britain, South America, Spain, Holland)
– Pierre does.
Whose job is in the kitchen? (dining room . . .)
– Pierre's is.

2   The detective is asking the hotel manager about the people at the hotel. Ask and answer in pairs:
Who is this? (Point at one photograph.)
– It's Consuela.
And what does she do?
– She's the maid.

3   Look at the objects on the right. Do you know their names? If not, look them up in a dictionary.
Now discuss them with your partner.
What's this?
– It's a knife.
Whose is it?
– It's Pierre's. He works in the kitchen.

Manuel is a waiter. He comes from Madrid.

Consuela is a maid, she cleans the hotel bedrooms. She comes from Brasilia.

Joe is an accountant. He comes from London.

Molly is the hotel receptionist, she works in the hotel lobby. She comes from Amsterdam.

6 What does the detective ask Consuela? Talk to your partner and decide.

7 Now listen to the tape and find out if your questions were correct. Write down the questions Mr Price asks each person.

8 Listen to the tape again and fill in the clues sheet.

1 The dead man was a ____.
2 The murderer killed him with a ____.
3 The murderer killed him on ____.
4 On Saturday evening
    Consuela was at the disco.
    Joe was ____.
    Pierre was ____.
    Manuel was ____.
    Molly was ____.
5 Who is the 6th person?
6 Who is Pedro?
7 On Saturday night Pedro was ____.
8 Why is Pedro in England?

Who killed the policeman?

9 Find the past of these verbs from the tape:
Regular   kill walk
Irregular   find hit come have

10 Roleplay
Work in pairs. Person **A** is Mr Price (the detective). Person **B** is Pedro. Look at your information below. Mr Price interviews Pedro. Start like this:
Mr Price: Pedro, where were you last night at 10 o'clock?

A

Ask Pedro about last night:
Where was he?
Who was he with?
What did he do?
When did he come back to the hotel?
Who did he see at the bar?
Where did they go?
What did he do then?

B

Last night you had a drink with Molly in the town, then you came back to the hotel at ten thirty. There was a Spanish policeman in the bar. He wanted to talk to you in his room. You were very frightened and you hit him with a bottle.

21

SUMMARY

Now you can :

talk about jobs
talk about possessions

KEY GRAMMAR
Question forms
Who works in the kitchen?
What does she do?
Where were you last night?
When did you find the body?
What did you do then?

Short forms
Pierre does.
Pierre's is.
She's a maid.

Past simple statements
I was at the disco.
We had a drink.
He came back here.

Possession
Whose job is in the kitchen?
Pierre's job is in the kitchen.

Vocabulary

come (came)	clue
find (found)	dead body
hit (hit)	detective
kill (killed)	murderer
murder (murdered)	policeman
	prison
guest	
maid	
receptionist	
waiter	

1 Make sentences about the objects, like this:

The cheaper umbrella is $\begin{Bmatrix} the\ same\ price \\ as\ expensive \end{Bmatrix}$ *as the ring.*

The pipe isn't as expensive as the jackets.

1 make-up/pipe
2 sweater/handbag
3 umbrella/hat and scarf
4 briefcase/glasses
5 briefcase/cufflinks

2 Choose four pictures and write sentences about each one, like this:

The ____ | is / are | the same price / as expensive / not as expensive | as the ____ .

3 Now take one of the sentences from Exercise 2, and ask your partner to guess the object.

It's not as expensive as the ____.

– Is it the ____?

Yes, it is./No. it isn't. It's the same colour as the ____.

4 Ask and answer in pairs.

Do you ever wear boots? (cufflinks, a hat, a scarf . . .)

– Yes, I do./No, I don't.

Do you ever use an umbrella? (make-up, a briefcase . . .)

– Yes, I do./No, I don't.

5 Listen to the tape and fill in the gaps.

A Oh, look at ____ two watches, aren't they lovely?
B ____ do you like?
A ____ very nice. I think I like . . .
B Do you like ____?
A Mm, yes, but I think I like ____ better. It's ____ gold, isn't it? And look at ____ rings! Now, they're lovely!
B Mm, I don't know, I think I like ____ better, over there, the plain gold ____ .
A But ____ are gold, they're white gold.
B Look, ____ do you like?
A I think I like ____ . Do you want to buy it for me?

6 Use the pictures to make dialogues, like this:

A Look at these ____ .
B Aren't they ____ . Which one do you like?
A I like the ____ one.
B Don't you like the ____ one?
A No.
B Why?
A Because it's expensive/made of ____/bad quality.

Use: *umbrellas, cameras, handbags, watches, bottles of wine.*

7 Match the two columns.
Then make sentences, like this:

These shoes are made of leather/plastic.

glasses	gold
skirt	plastic
shoes	wool
case	silver
ring	leather
jackets	cloth
necklace	crystal

8 Write the name of an object on a piece of paper. The teacher collects the papers, then gives them out again, one to each person. Look at your paper and say to your partner:

What have you got for your birthday?

– I've got a ____ .

Do you need a ____?

– Yes, I do./No, I don't.

What (else) do you need?

– I need a ____ .

Now find the object you need. Choose a new partner and ask:

Have you got a ____?

– Yes, I have./No, I haven't.

Talk to people and find the object you need.

9 Write about Marriot's sale. Choose three objects.
In Marriot's sale there is a ____ . It's ____ and it's made of ____ . It costs ____ . . .

SUMMARY

Now you can :

compare similar things
talk about what something is made of

KEY GRAMMAR
Question forms
Do you ever use make-up?
Which one do you like?

Present simple statements
The umbrella is the same price as the ring.
It's as expensive as the ring.
Is isn't as expensive as the suitcase.
The ring's made of silver.

Determiners
this (one)   that (one)   these   those

Vocabulary

need	cloth	beautiful
made of	gold	handsome
briefcase	leather	lovely
camera	plastic	plain
cufflinks	quality	popular
make-up	silver	pretty
pipe	wool	smart
suitcase		
umbrella		
watch		

Gifts for all the family

For the older man

A £13.00

B £8.50

Does he need a new umbrella? These are very smart. **A** is better quality than **B** but it is also more expensive.

For the wine lover. The Chablis is as good as the Bordeaux: they're both about the same price.

£6.50

£6.75

£22.00

A very popular gift for the pipe-smoker.

£27.99

These handsome cufflinks are made of 18-carat gold.

For the younger man

More expensive than the suitcase, it's made of soft leather. A smart executive briefcase.

For the travelling man. Made of good quality plastic, it's the same colour as the briefcase.

£27.99

£53.50

£55.99

£55.99

B £45.00

A £60.00

Why not give him a camera. In Marriot's super sale the 35 mm is the same price as the Polaroid.

A is for the casual look, made of leather, **B** for the smart look, made of heavy cotton.

For the older woman

These beautiful glasses are a lovely gift, and they're not as expensive as the sweater.

Two Italian handbags: **B** is made of soft leather, **A** is made of cloth. **A** is cheaper than **B**

A £9.50

£35.00 **B**

£27.99

£129.00

B

A £83.50

£35.00

Two lovely watches for today's woman. **A** is made of silver, **B** of gold.

This lovely sweater is made of 100% Cashmere wool.

For the younger woman

£20.00

Does she use make-up? Buy two bottles of perfume from Marriot's and get this set for only £20.00.

Give her this lovely hat and scarf set. The hat is the same colour as the scarf.

£13.00

£55.99

Stay warm in winter! Made of leather, these boots have got a wool lining.

£8.50

Just a little gift? How about this pretty silver ring. Inexpensive, but very nice.

Marriot's

22

CROSSING THE CHANNEL

More and more people cross the Channel every year. There are a lot of ferries every day. They are fast and they're not expensive. They're also very comfortable. You can always get something to eat in the restaurant or a drink at the bar. You can buy cheap duty free goods in the shop. Here we look at three routes across the Channel from Hamburg.

Routes to the Lake District with Seatrips					
Hamburg–Harwich Ostend–Folkestone Calais–Dover					
Hamburg to port (kms)	Number of ships per week in summer	Number of cars per week	Length of sailing time	Price (car +4 people)	English port to lakes (km)
Hamburg 0 kms	7	1,000	20 hours	£270	Harwich 420 kms
Ostend 682 kms	25 approx.	3,500	3½ hours	£73	Folkestone 550 kms
Calais 766 kms	90 approx.	13,000	1½ hours	£73	Dover 560 kms

1 Compare the three routes. Fill in the gaps.
The table above shows three routes from Hamburg to the English Lake District. All routes are by car and ferry. The Hamburg to Harwich ferry costs ____ than the others because the sea journey is much ____, but there is ____ time on the road. The other two routes are ____, but the journey from Ostend to Folkestone takes ____ than the journey from Calais to Dover. In England, Harwich is ____ the Lake District, but there are motorways from Folkestone and Dover and the journey is ____ and ____.

2 Compare the Ostend to Folkestone crossing with the Calais to Dover crossing.
Which crossing is longer? (shorter, faster, slower, cheaper, more expensive)
– *The Ostend to Folkestone crossing is longer than the Calais to Dover crossing.*
Which crossing has more/fewer ships/cars per week, Calais to Dover or Ostend to Folkestone?
– *The Calais to Dover crossing has ____ cars than the ____.*

3 Look at the table on the left and complete these sentences.
1 In summer the ____ is better than in winter.
2 In ____ the crossing is better than in ____.
3 In spring the weather is ____ in summer.
4 In winter the crossing is worse than in ____.
5 In spring the crossing is better than in ____.
6 In winter the traffic is better than in ____.
7 In spring the traffic is ____ in summer.
8 In spring the weather is ____ in winter.

Which is better? Which is worse?				
This table gives you information about a holiday in Britain at different times of the year.				
	spring	summer	autumn	winter
traffic	***	*	***	***
weather	***	***	**	*
crossing	**	***	**	*
*** = very good ** = average * = bad				

In winter the weather is worse than in summer, but the traffic is better.

4 When is a good time for a holiday in England?
Look at the table and make sentences in pairs.
– *Go in the winter because the traffic is better than in the summer.*
– *Don't go in the winter because the weather is worse than in the summer.*

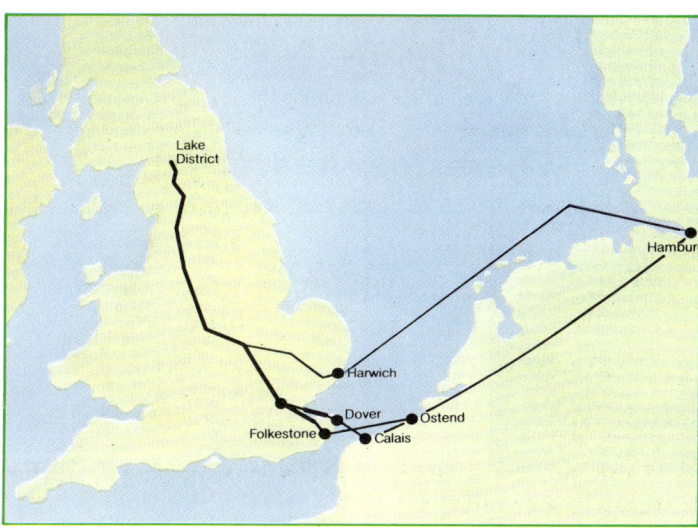

5 Listen to the tape and fill in the gaps.

A ____ Britain on holiday?

B Oh, yes ____ to Britain.

A Where have you been?

B Well, last year ____ to the Lake District, but ____ to Scotland and Ireland. We always go in summer because the ____ .

A Yes, but ____ .

B Yes, that's right. But it's the same in every country.

6 Ask and answer in pairs.

When did you go on holiday last year, and why?

– I went in June because the weather is better than in ____ .

– I didn't go in ____ because the ____ is worse than in ____ .

Where did you go?

– I went to ____ because ____ .

7 Roleplay

Person **A** asks questions from Box **A**, Person **B** answers them. Use *when, why, which, how much* and *how long*.

A *When is a good time to go to London, spring or summer ____ .*

B *Spring is ____ .*

SUMMARY

Now you can :

talk about where you go on holiday
give reasons
give advice

KEY GRAMMAR
Question forms

When did you go . . . ?
Where did you go . . . ?
Why did you go . . . ?
Why didn't you go . . . ?

Past simple

I didn't go because . . .
I went in September.

Imperative

Go in the summer.
Don't go in the winter.

Comparison

better than . . .
worse than . . .

Vocabulary

go (went)	crossing
show (showed)	ferry
take (took)	journey
	route
weather	traffic
spring	more ⎫
summer	fewer ⎭ ships
autumn	
winter	

A

> You want to go to London on holiday. Ask about a good time to go (spring or summer), and why, about a good crossing from Hamburg, the price and how long it is.

B

> You are a travel agent. You think the spring is a better time to visit London than the summer because it has good weather and there are fewer tourists in spring. Ostend to Folkestone is a better crossing than Hamburg to Harwich because it is shorter and cheaper. It takes 3½ hours and costs £27 per person.

8 Which route do you like? Why? Look at the map and the tables. Write your reason:

I like the ____ because there are ____ and ____ . I know the ____ is worse than ____ but the ____ is better.

23

51

REVISION

1 Letter-writing

Write to Patty Dean. Tell her about yourself, your
town and your family.

24

3 Conversation corner

Ask and answer in pairs:
What time did you get up?
– I got up at ____ .
What did you have for breakfast?
– I had ____ .
How did you come to school?
– I came by/on ____ .
*What would you like to have for
lunch/dinner?*
– I'd like ____ .

4 What is Jürgen? Where does he work?

 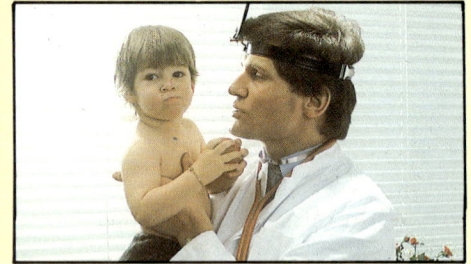

Jürgen is a doctor, he works in a hospital.

policeman	school
driver	bus company
teacher	hotel
secretary	airport
accountant	police station
engineer	office

8 Here are some verbs from Units 19–23. What are they?

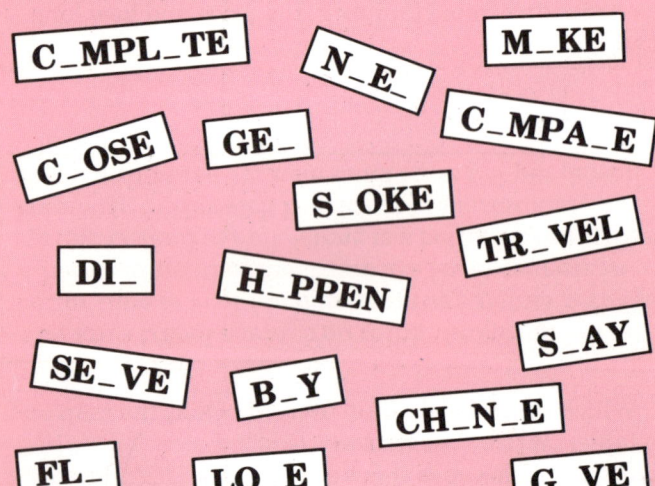

C_MPL_TE   N_E_   M_KE
C_OSE   GE_   C_MPA_E
S_OKE
DI_   H_PPEN   TR_VEL
S_AY
SE_VE   B_Y
CH_N_E
FL_   LO_E   G_VE

Write the past forms of these verbs:

happen   have   is   make   lose   talk   look   are
change   do   work

Now complete these sentences, using the verbs on the
left and above.

1. I don't ____ any help.
2. I have to ____ English.
3. I want to ____ some food.
4. Do you ____ cigarettes or cigars?
5. Please ____ the door.
6. In 1976 she ____ in a factory.
7. They ____ do it. I ____ .
8. This morning I ____ my watch, but I found it again
   this afternoon.

2 Look at the photographs. Which sentences on the right are true and which are false?

Francoise left school ten years ago.

After she left school she lived in Lyons for a year.

Before she went to Lyons she lived in Nice.

Her first job was in Paris.

She now works in Brussels.

1 She works in Paris.
2 She was at school in Lyons.
3 When she lived in Nice she was at school.
4 She wasn't at school twelve years ago.
5 She was at school eight years ago.
6 She isn't working in France.
7 She was at school before she went to Lyons.
8 She lived in Lyons after she lived in Nice.

5 Game

Think of something in the room. Other people ask you questions, like this:

Is it big/small? (size)
– Yes, it is./No, it isn't.
Is it red/brown? (colour)
– Yes, it is./No, it isn't.
Is it a triangle/square? (shape)
– Yes, it is./No, it isn't.
Is it made of wood/plastic?
   (material: cotton, wool, metal)
– Yes, it is./No, it isn't.
Is it a ___? (name)
– Yes, it is./No, it isn't.

6 Words and figures

Ask and answer in pairs.
Which is larger, (e) or (i)?
– ___ is the same as ___./___ is larger than ___.

(a) 10.5   (b) 105   (c) .105   (d) 10½   (e) 1 + 6 + 9
(f) 5 + 10 + 1   (g) 7 + 19 − 8   (h) 18 + 2 − 3   (i) 18 − 1 + 0

London Paddington to Minchhampton

Mondays to Fridays

		☒			☒		☒	☒				☒	
London Paddington	dep	07.20	08.20	09.00	09.20	11.20	13.20	15.20	16.20	17.00	17.20	18.00	19.20
Minchhampton	arr	09.10	10.10	10.20	11.10	13.10	15.10	17.10	18.10	18.20	19.10	19.20	21.10

		☒			☒		☒						
Minchhampton	dep	06.45	07.00	07.45	08.00	08.45	10.45	12.45	14.45	16.45	17.45	18.00	18.45	20.45
London Paddington	arr	08.35	08.20	09.35	09.20	10.35	12.35	14.35	16.35	18.35	19.35	19.20	20.35	22.35

7 Look at the timetable and ask and answer in pairs.
How long does it take from ___ to ___?
Which train takes longer, the ___ or the ___?

9 Puzzle

Do you know these words?
Complete the diagram and do the puzzle.
What is the sport in the circles?

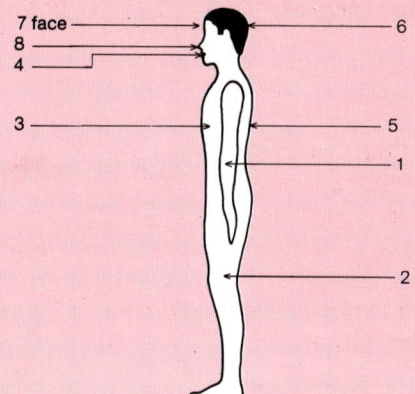

7 face
8
4
6
3
5
1
2

1
2
3
4
5
6
7
8

The New Photofax 2000

It's easy! A child can use it.

How do you use it? The pictures tell you.

on off	off/on button	Turn it on/off.	hand with a cross	Don't touch.
square with a cross		Wait! It's not ready.	an arrow		Put more paper in the machine.
circle with a tick		Start.	rectangle		Turn the machine off. Clean it.
triangle		Stop! Don't use. Read the instructions.	cylinder		Put more ink in the machine.
repair man		Stop! Don't use. Call the repair man.	dial		Choose the number of copies.

* All red signs = something is wrong.

1 Ask and answer in pairs.
What do you call a ○ *in English?* (✓ ✗ ▭ △ ◎ ⇒)
– It's a circle.

2 Ask and answer in pairs.
What does a square with a cross ⊠ *mean?*
– It means wait.

Instructions

⊠	When you see this sign, wait. You mustn't use the machine. It's not ready.
△	When you see this sign, you must stop. Look for other signs.
🧍	When you see this sign, you must stop. Call the repair man.
▭	When you see this sign, you must turn the machine off. Someone must clean it.
🖐	When you see this sign, you mustn't touch the machine. It's hot.

---

3 Ask and answer in pairs.
What do you do when you see the square with a cross ⊠ *?*
– You must ____./You mustn't ____.

4 What must you do when you see these signs?
Match the signs and the instructions.

1 You must wear a strong hat.
2 You mustn't walk on the grass.
3 You mustn't smoke.
4 You must be quiet.
5 You must wear dark glasses.
6 You mustn't drive fast.

Now make commands from these instructions, like this:
Wear a strong hat.   Don't walk on the grass.

5 Listen to the tape and complete this form.
Someone is calling Photofax Ltd. Write the name, address, telephone number and serial number of the machine.

> **What is wrong? Tick the signs.**
>
> ⊠ ✓ △ 🧍 🖐 ⇒ ▭ ◎ ◔
>
> Name _____
> Address _____
> Telephone number _____
> Serial number of machine ____

---

6 Roleplay
You have a Photofax 2000. There is something wrong with your machine. You call Photofax. Give your name, address, telephone number and the serial number. Which lights are on? Tell them. Follow the example below. Write the details of your address, telephone number and serial number, and then act the telephone call with your partner.

A Hello, is ____?
B Yes, ____.
A Can I ____?
B Yes, what is your ____?
A ____.
B And your ____?
A ____.
B What's the ____?
A ____.
B Thank you. Which ____?
A The ____.
B Is the ____?
A No, but the ____.
B Have you ____?
A No, I ____.
B Turn ____. Don't ____.

25

SUMMARY

Now you can:

read and give instructions

KEY GRAMMAR
Question forms
What does ____ mean?
What do you call a ____?
What do you do when ____?
What must you do when ____?

Imperative
Put more paper in the machine.
Don't touch.

Direct objects
Turn it on.
Clean it.

Modal verb
must

When clauses
When you see this sign you
    must stop.

Vocabulary
call (called)
clean (cleaned)
mean (meant)
put (put)
start (started)
stop (stopped)
touch (touched)
turn on/off (turned on/off)

arrow	rectangle
circle	square
cross	triangle
cylinder	

A change in lifestyle

Three years ago Neil Travers had a bad accident. It was at night and the weather was very bad. He could not see very well, and his car hit a tree. Now Neil can't use his legs.

1 Find the past of these verbs in the text.
can   have   hit   is
(They are all irregular.)

Neil's wife, Caroline, tells us about the difference in their lives now.

"Neil and I worked. We both taught at a large school in London. Neil taught languages. He liked football a lot, and other sports too. Swimming, for example. Then he had the accident. At first, he was very unhappy and he needed a lot of help. I stayed at home with him. It's much better now. He can do a lot of things, but there are also things he can't do."

2 These sentences are in the past.
Write them in the present.

Neil and I worked.
We both taught at a large school.
He liked football a lot.
He was very unhappy and he needed a lot of help.

3 Ask and answer in pairs.
Where did Neil work three years ago?
– He worked ____.
What/Neil/teach/three/ago?
What/Neil/like/ago?

Where did you live three years ago?
– I lived ____.
Where/you/work/ago?
What/you/do/ago?

4 Look at the photographs on the right. Now write two sentences, like this:
Neil can ____ and ____.
He can't ____ or ____.

5 Draw a box, like the one below, and write numbers in it.

top left corner		top right corner
6		**5**
	middle **2**	
4		**3**
bottom left corner		bottom right corner

Show it to your partner for ten seconds, then ask:
Can you remember the number in the top right corner?
– Yes, I can. It's five./No, I can't. What is it?

6 Ask and answer in pairs.
What languages can you speak?
– I can speak ____, but I can't speak ____.
What can you cook?
– I can cook ____, but I can't cook ____.
What sports can you do?
– I can ____.

7 Listen to the tape. Complete the sentences.
Neil couldn't ____.
He couldn't ____ and he couldn't ____.
Listen again.
Neil can do four things. What are they?

There are some things Neil can do, and there are some things he can't do.

He can help in the house, but he can't climb stairs.

He can use a computer, but he can't take a bus.

He can teach, but he can't play football.

He can go to the theatre, but he can't swim.

What can a Buddhist eat? (Tick √)	pork	ham	bacon	beef	fish	vegetables	fruit	beer	wine	milk
Hindu										
Muslim										
Buddhist										

8 Work in groups. Complete this table.
Check your answers with other groups, like this:
Can a Hindu eat pork?
– Yes, he can./No, he can't.

9 Now listen to the tape to check your answers.

10 Write about the diet of a Muslim, a Hindu or a Buddhist.
A Muslim can eat ____, but he can't eat ____. He can drink ____.

SUMMARY

Now you can :

say what you can and can't do

KEY GRAMMAR
Question forms
Can you remember?
What languages can you speak?

Modal verbs
can/can't/could/couldn't
He can do a lot of things. He can't use his legs.
He could teach. He couldn't see very well.

Vocabulary
help (helped)
hit (hit)
remember (remembered)
see (saw)
stay (stayed)
take (+ bus) (took)
teach (taught)

accident

Richard Darwin Keynes has got a very famous great grandfather – Charles Darwin, the naturalist. Richard Darwin is a scientist, too, and he also looks a bit like his great grandfather.

Families often look alike, and they sometimes do the same things. Many children of actors and actresses have become stars. Some children of authors write books, and children of sportsmen and women are often good at sports.

And in our towns and villages there are always family shops; butcher's, baker's, newsagent's; sometimes the same family has owned them for a hundred years or more.

Are you like your great grandfather?

1 Have you got any famous grandparents/great grandparents?
– Yes, I have. My grand____ was ____.
– No, I haven't. My grand____ worked in/as a ____.

2 Can you think of any family shops in your town?
Write the names:
Now ask the class:
Do you know ____ (name)? It's a butcher's. (baker's etc)

George Brown is 56. He's got grey hair and brown eyes.

Melanie Brown is 46. She's got red hair and green eyes.

Geoff Brown is 21. He's got brown hair and brown eyes.

Julia Brown is 19. She's got red hair and brown eyes.

Geoff and Julia have got the same eyes, but their hair is different.

Geoff Brown looks like his father because they've got the same eyes, nose and mouth. He doesn't look like his mother.

Julia Brown looks like her father because they've got the same eyes and mouth. She also looks like her mother. They have the same hair and nose.

3 Describe one of the Browns, like this:
Mr Brown is quite old. He's got a large nose. His mouth and his ears are also large. He's got grey hair and brown eyes.
Use these words:
nose (long, large, small)   *face* (thin, wide, small)
mouth (large, small, thin)   *hair* (colour, long, short)
ears (large, small)   *eyes* (colour, large)

4 Ask and answer in pairs.
Does ____ look like ____?
– Yes. They have the same ____ and the same ____.
– No. They have the same ____ but their ____ are different.

5 Ask and answer in pairs.
Who do you look like?
– I look like my ____ because our ____ is/are the same.
– I don't look like my ____ because our ____ is/are different.

6 Compare people in your class.

	hair eyes feet dress jacket	is/are	the same	colour length size	as
____'s					____'s. mine.

7 Look at the photographs on the right and complete the table. Work in groups of four.
Ask and answer like this:
Who is Peter's mother?
– I think Peter's mother is ____ because their ____ is/are the same.
How many in the group think Peter's mother is Sheila? One? Then write the number one.

	Sheila	Jane	Mary	Sue
Peter				
Jill				
Joyce				
Robert				

8 Write sentences about the four mothers and their children.

9 Listen to the tape and answer the questions.
1 Where is the woman?
2 Who do you think she is talking to?
3 The woman went into the post office. Where was her little girl?
4 What colour is the woman's hair?
Now write a description of the little girl for the police notice. Start like this:
Alice is seven, she's got ____ .

Sheila

Jane

Mary

Sue

Peter

Jill

Joyce

Robert

SUMMARY

Now you can :

talk about similarities

KEY GRAMMAR
Question forms
Have you got any famous grandparents?
Who do you look like?

General statements (present)
He's got brown hair and brown eyes.
She looks like her mother because they've got the same nose.
They've got the same nose but their eyes are different.
I can't find my daughter.

Possessives
His eyes are the same colour as mine.

Vocabulary

look like	face
	hair
same	mouth
different	nose
ears	
eyes	

THE CASPAR INTERVIEW

Steven Casper *is talking to Anna, a Hungarian dancer. She came to London thirty years ago.*

28

1   Anna is speaking about her early life before she came to England.
Listen and fill in the gaps.

Anna: I was born on a ____ in Hungary.

Caspar: On a ____?

Anna: Yes, it's true. My poor mother. She was on her way to Budapest, to my ____ house. It was early in the morning, on the ____ of January, 193..., ah, but you don't want to know the year, do you?

Caspar: So you grew up in Hungary?

Anna: Yes and no. I lived in Hungary for five years, and then I went to school in Paris. My father was a ____, and my mother played the piano. Oh, she played the piano very well. And in Paris I met my ____ husband.

Caspar: Was he French?

Anna: No, that was my ____ husband.

Name _____

Date of birth _____

Place of birth _____

Name of school _____

Town _____

Married?   Yes/No

2   Complete the form on the left for your partner.
Ask and answer in pairs.

When/where were you born?   – I was born on ____. (date)
                            – I was born in ____. (place)

Where did you go to school?   – I went to school in ____.

Are you married?

Life was very hard for Anna when she came to London. Her husband died and she didn't have any money. She couldn't speak English and she didn't have any friends. For a time she lived alone. Then she met Marie-Chantal. Marie-Chantal was French and was a dancer. Anna spoke French. Now, thirty years later they are both very famous.

60

3 Look at the last text and make questions.
In pairs, ask and answer questions, like this:
1 What happened to Anna's husband?   He died.
2 Could Anna ____ English?   No, she ____.
3 Did Anna have ____?   No, she ____.
4 Why ____ life hard for ____?   Because she ____.
5 What ____ Marie-Chantal do?   She ____.
6 Where ____ Marie-Chantal ____ from?   She ____ from ____.
7 What have ____ become?   They ____.

4 Listen to the tape. Marie-Chantal talks about Anna in those early days. Write the answers to the questions below.
1 Anna couldn't do three things. What were they?
2 Who was at the door?
3 What did he speak?
4 What did Anna speak?
5 What did Marie-Chantal speak?

5 Now ask your partner questions.
1 What happened to Anna's husband?
2 Where was Anna born?
3 Where did she go to school?
4 What was her father?
5 What did her mother do?
6 How many husbands did she have?

6 Look at this text. Anna is talking.

'Living in London is easier now, but I am still learning English. The grammar is difficult, but the pronunciation is worse. And I don't understand English spelling. But at school I was always bad at languages, I was only good at music.'

Here is a list of school subjects. Match the subject with the definition:

geography	French, English, German
history	the study of living things
languages	the study of the world
mathematics	the science of figures
biology	the study of books
literature	the study of the past

7 What are these subjects in your language?
Physics, chemistry, economics, computer science, music, sport.
Can you think of any others? Remember, you can ask, 'How do you say ____ in English?'

8 Ask and answer in pairs.
Were you good at history? (maths, literature, sport, music, biology . . .)
– { *Yes, I was, but I was bad at ____.*
   { *No, I wasn't, but I was good at ____.*
What were you very good/bad at when you were at school?
– I was very good/bad at ____.

9 Write about yourself.
I am learning ____ (English/French/Italian etc). I think the ____ is difficult but the ____ is ____ (better/worse). I don't understand ____. At school I learnt ____. I was good at ____ but I was bad at ____.

28

The Lord Mayor's Parade

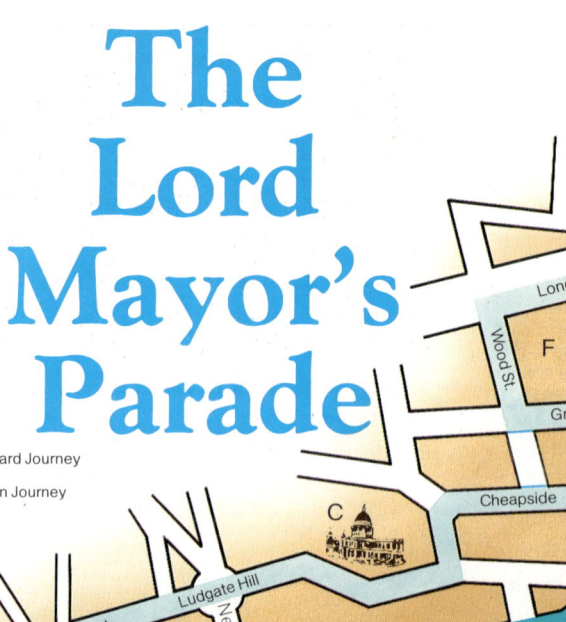

Outward Journey
Return Journey

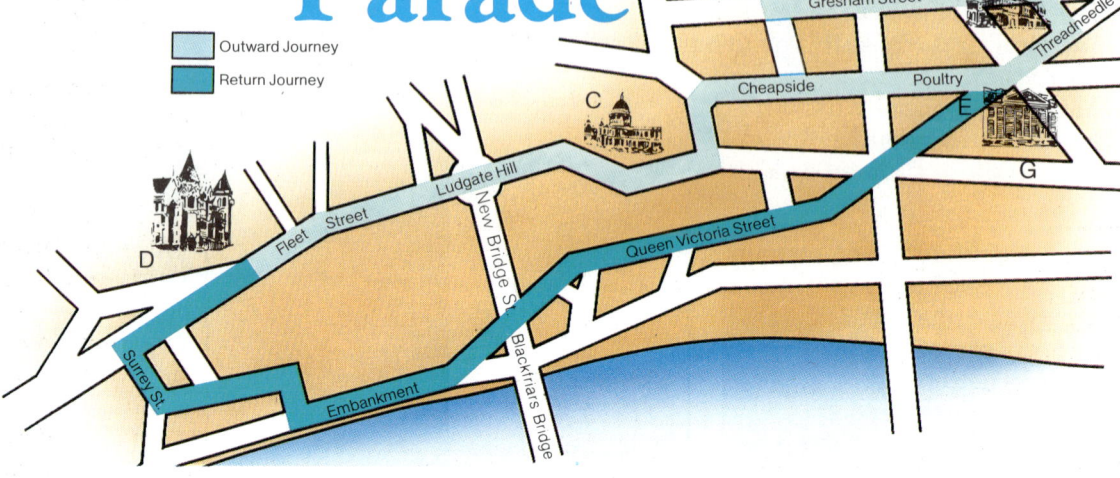

Every November the people of London choose a new mayor and there is a colourful parade through the streets. This is called the Lord Mayor's Parade and thousands of people come to watch it. There are always a lot of bands and people from the Army, Navy and Air Force. There are also a lot of people from different trades, for example, builders, bakers, grocers and carpenters. The Lord Mayor rides in a coach near the end of the parade.

Programme

11.10 am	The parade starts from London Wall. It turns into Wood Street, and then into Gresham Street. On the left is the Guildhall.
11.20 am	The parade continues along Threadneedle Street. It passes the Bank of England. It then goes to Mansion House. The Lord Mayor lives here.
11.30 am	The parade goes down Cheapside and around St Paul's.
11.45 am	The parade continues down Ludgate Hill and along Fleet Street, to the Courts of Justice. Here, the Lord Mayor has lunch.
1.15 pm	After lunch, the parade continues to The Strand and turns left at Surrey Street. It then returns along the river. It passes Blackfriars Bridge on the right and arrives at Mansion House at 1.50 pm.

1 Look at the map and read the programme.
What are **A**, **B**, **C**, **D**, **E**, **F** and **G** on the map?
The Guildhall _____
The Courts of Justice _____
St Paul's Cathedral _____
Mansion House _____
The Bank of England _____
The start of the parade _____
The end of the parade _____

2 Answer these questions.
Where does the parade start?
When does the parade start?
Where is The Guildhall? (The Bank of England, St Paul's Cathedral . . .)
Where does the Lord Mayor have lunch?

3 Listen to the tape and follow the route from Blackfriars to the Guildhall. Now tell your partner how to get from the Guildhall to Blackfriars. Are your instructions correct?

4 Make dialogues. Fill in the gaps from the map.
A Excuse me. How do I get to ____?
B Where are you now?
A I'm at ____.
B You go along ____, you turn left/ then right, you go up ____.
____ is on your left/right.
A How long does it take?
B About ____.
A Thank you.

5 Choose two places from the list below, write down the route from one to the other, then ask your partner:
How do I get to ____ from ____?
Use these words and phrases:
Go along ____ Street.
Turn right.
Turn left.
The ____ is on your right/left.

> The Royal Courts of Justice
> St Paul's
> Blackfriars
> Mansion House Station

Does your partner agree with you?

6 Ask and answer in pairs.
How long does it take from your house to the shops? (station, your work, airport . . .)
– *It takes about ____.*
How long does it take you to come here from your home?
– *It takes about ____.*

7 Write sentences.
____ lives nearer the station than I do.
I live nearer the ____ than he/she does.
It takes me less/more time to go to the ____ than it takes ____.
It takes me a longer/shorter time to come here than it does ____.

29

8 Look at this sentence from the passage:
There are also a lot of people from different trades, for example, builders, bakers, grocers and carpenters.
Make sentences about tradespeople from the two columns:
A builder makes buildings.

builder		bread
carpenter		holidays
greengrocer		vegetables
butcher		and fruit
baker	makes	meat
farmer	sells	interesting
cook	grows	meals
travel		tables
agent		buildings

Dear Carrie,

This is my uncle. Two years ago he left Germany and went to England. We have never had a letter from him, or a telephone call. Please put his photograph in your magazine.

He is very tall, about 1.93 m, and he's got grey hair. He speaks English very well and is an engineer. Perhaps he is working for an English company. We don't know.

He's about 60, he isn't married and he hasn't got any children. My family wants to see him again. Can you help?
Yours sincerely

Bianka

Dear Bianka,
Thank you for sending me your uncle's picture. I'm returning it to you. You didn't tell us his name. Please call me on this number – 01 246 8811.

Carrie

1 Letter-writing

Write a letter to Carrie about a relation (an aunt, uncle or cousin). Describe him/her.

2 Read this passage then fill in the form below.

I was born on the first day of the third month of the year, ten years after the end of the Second World War. My mother and father had two daughters; my sister was born a year before me. My parents are both still alive, my father works in a hospital and my mother is a teacher. My sister's a teacher, too. I'm still studying. My sister is married, and I'm getting married next month. We live in Edinburgh; my parents were born there and so were we.

Sex (male/female) _____
Date of birth _____
Place of birth _____
Married/single _____
Occupation _____
Family _____

6 Puzzle

Are they the same or are they different?

Ask your partner: Is **A** the same as **B**?
– No, **B**'s different because it hasn't got any circles, but **B** is the same as **I** because they've both got three squares

A □ □ ○   B □ □ □   C ○ ○ △

D △ □ ○   E ○ ○ □   F □ ○ □

G △ △ □   H △ △ ○   I □ □ □

J △ △ □   K □ ○ ○   L △ ○ △

7 Who do you look like in your family? Why?
Write about yourself and your family.

8 Here are some verbs from Units 25 to 29. What are they?

T_RN   S_OP   GR_W   D__VE   H_LP   N_ED   A__IVE   T_UC_   CO_T_NUE   W__T   R__URN   ME_T   R_DE

3 Now answer these questions.

1 Which month was the writer born in?
2 How old is the writer now?
3 How old is the sister now?
4 What does she do?
5 What does the father do?
6 What does the mother do?

4 Puzzle

Find the names of ten sports from this word square then make sentences, like this:
I can ____, but I can't ____.

```
L C R I C K E T S S
O T V V L E G C G W
T E N N I S J Y L I
M S X A M P Q C V M
F O O T B A L L J M
G M C Z I R T I L I
K N Y J N L B N L N
O J O G G I N G O G
F L G S K A T I N G
W X A E R O B I C S
```

You can find words going across or down.

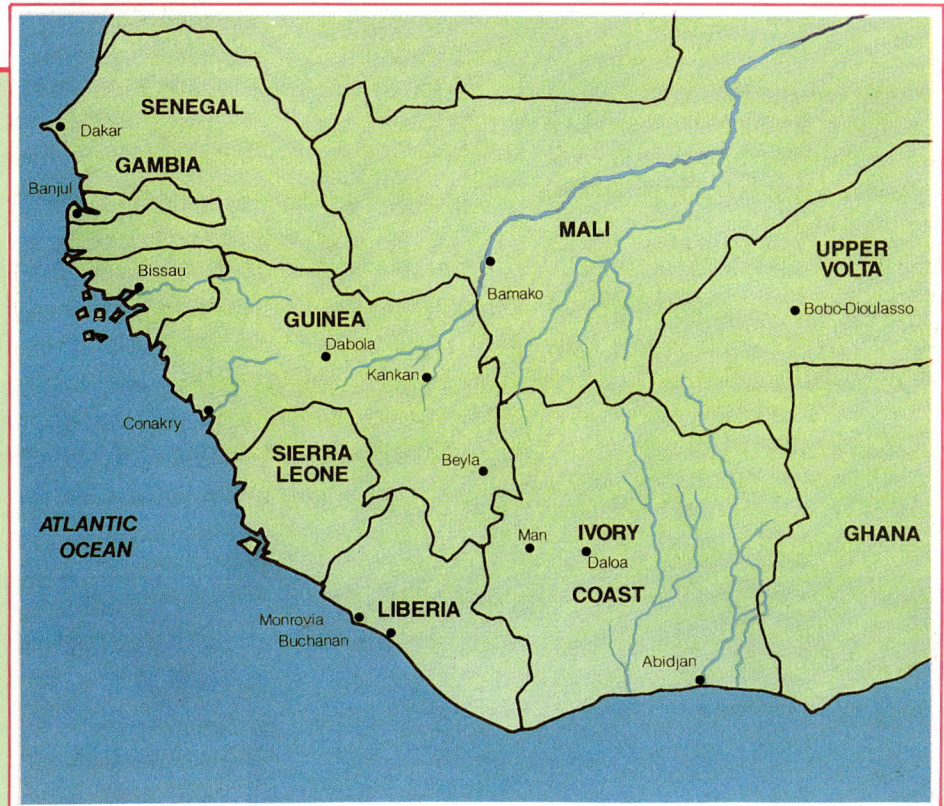

5 Look at the map

Find a town and find out some facts about it.
It it on a river? Is it near the sea? Which part of the country is it in?

Now ask your partner the questions.

30

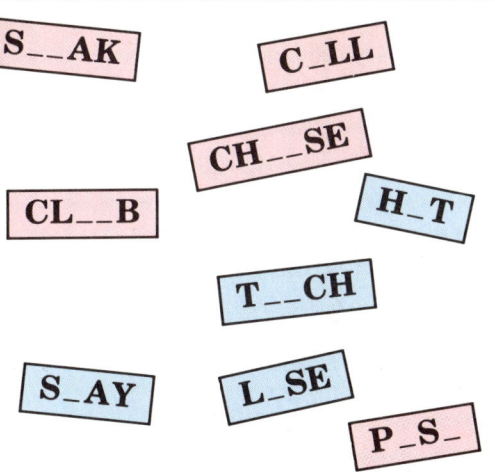

Write the blue verbs in the past.
Now complete these sentences, using the past forms of the blue verbs.

1 She ____ in a children's school when she was young.
2 They ____ at six o'clock.
3 The murderer ____ the girl with a bottle.
4 We had no petrol and the car ____ .
5 I ____ up in the country, then moved to London.

9 Puzzle

All the words in this puzzle are the names of clothes. Find all the names across, using the word down, and the clues.

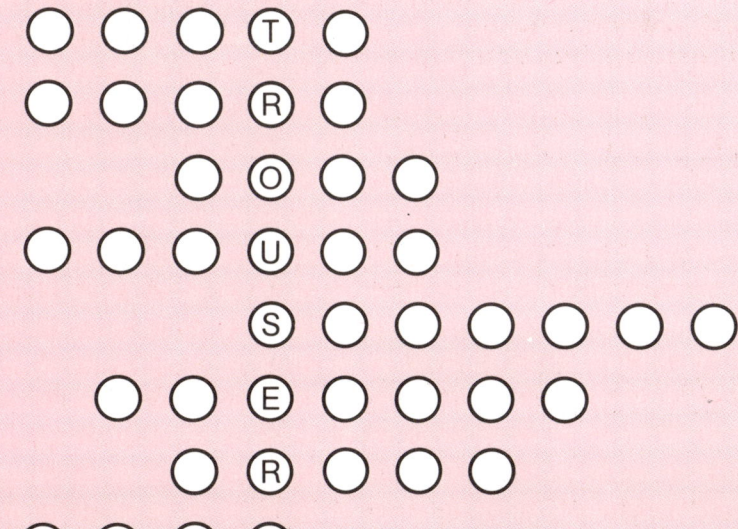

Clues:

summer shoes; winter shoes; usually made of wool; we wear them on our feet; a woman's shirt; what we wear over our clothes; men wear a ____ and tie; formal women's wear.

English people like a good cup of tea – in bed or in the bath, on a train or a plane, in England or France, in China or Brazil. They drink an average of four cups a day.

1   English people like drinking tea. What do French people like drinking? (Scottish, Polish, German, Danish, Turkish, American...)

2   Class survey
How many people in your class like beer? Write their names in the table.

How do you make a good cup of tea?

beer	wine	whisky	tea	Coca-Cola	brandy	champagne	coffee

3   Make sentences like this:

John/England/4/cup/tea
John is from England. He drinks an average of four cups of tea a day.

1   Bruce/Scotland/2/glass/whisky
2   Ronald/USA/5/glass/Coca-Cola
3   Petra/USSR/3/glass/vodka
4   Odile/France/4/glass/wine
5   Hermann/Germany/4/glass/beer

4   How do you make a good cup of tea? Match the pictures to the instructions. The pictures are in the correct order.

1   Now fill the teapot with boiling water. The water must still be boiling.
2   First boil the water.
3   Some people prefer lemon.
4   Leave it for about four minutes.
5   Put the lid on the teapot and cover it with a tea cosy.
6   Boil the water again.
7   Next, put a little milk and/or sugar in the cups.
8   Put the tea leaves into the pot. Put one teaspoon per person and one for the pot.
9   Then pour a little boiling water into the teapot. Warm the pot and pour it out again.
10   Finally pour the tea through the strainer, into the cup, and stir. (You can also use tea bags, but they're not as good.)

Ingredients	Equipment
water	kettle (saucepan)
tea (leaves or bags)	teaspoon
milk	cup
sugar	saucer
(lemon)	teapot
	(strainer)
	(tea cosy)

5 Complete the following with prepositions.
Fill the kettle ___ water and put it ___ the cooker. Boil the water, then pour a little boiling water ___ the teapot to warm it. Pour the water ___ the teapot. Boil the water again. Put some tea ___ the pot, then put the water ___ the pot, stir, and cover it ___ a tea cosy. Leave the tea ___ a few minutes. Put a little milk and/or sugar ___ the cups. Pour the tea ___ the strainer ___ the cups and stir.

6 Here are some instructions for making an omelette. Put them into the correct order, and join the sentences with the words below. (Look up any new words in a dictionary.)
1 ___ break two or three eggs into a bowl ___ beat them with a fork.
2 ___ , turn the omelette over ___ cook for a few more minutes.
3 ___ put some oil in a pan and heat it.
4 ___ , add a little milk or water, and some salt and pepper to the eggs.
5 Pour the eggs into the pan ___ cook for a few minutes.

and/Finally/Next/and/Then/ First/and

7 Work in groups. Make pairs with a word from each box, like this: *milk and sugar*. Use a dictionary if necessary.

milk	knife	fork	vinegar
tea	bread	pepper	coffee
cup	fish	sugar	saucer
salt	oil	butter	chips

Make sentences with the pairs:
I like milk and sugar in tea.

8 Ask and answer in pairs.
Do you prefer tea or coffee?
– I don't like either tea or coffee./I prefer tea to coffee.

tea with milk/tea with lemon
wine/beer
red wine/white wine
English beer/German beer
whisky/vodka
black coffee/white coffee

9 Listen to the tape.
What would the man like to drink? Now make similar dialogues with your partner three times, using this information.
1 Repeat after the tape.
2 You want milk and no sugar.
3 You'd like coffee with milk only.

10 How do you make a cup of coffee?
1 Work alone. Look at the table. Write down your way of making coffee.

Ingredients:	coffee
	_____
	_____
	_____
Equipment:	_____
	_____
	_____
	_____
	_____
Instructions:	1 _____
	2 _____
	3 _____
	4 _____

2 Work with a partner. Find out if you make coffee in the same way. (Don't look at each other's instructions.) What is the same/ different about your ways of making coffee? Choose the best one.
3 Now work in groups of four. Choose the best way of making coffee in your group.
4 Talk about making coffee in the class. How many different ways of making coffee are there?
5 Write a different way of making coffee (not your way). Write the instructions like Exercise 5.

SUMMARY

Now you can:

talk about what you like drinking
make sequences

KEY GRAMMAR
Question forms
What do French people like drinking?
How do you make a good cup of tea?
Do you prefer tea or coffee?

Present simple statements
John drinks an average of four cups of tea a day.
I prefer tea to coffee.
I don't like either tea or coffee.

Connectors
first
next
then
and
finally

Vocabulary

boil	beer
cover	brandy
fill	champagne
pour	Coca-Cola
prefer	coffee
stir	tea
	vodka
cosy	whisky
cup	wine
kettle	
strainer	
saucer	
teapot	
teaspoon	

These days money buys less than it did before. People are usually more careful with their money. People are buying less. Food, for example, costs more these days.

	Ten years ago	Today
Butter (250 g)	24p	52p
Eggs (12)	35p	94p
Tea (125 g)	9p	55p
Potatoes (kg)	3–6p	12–20p
Milk (litre)	11p	42p
Bread (large)	10p	50p
Cheese (½ kg)	37p	£1–£1.40p

VALUE FOR MONEY

Ten years ago butter cost half as much as today for 250 grams. Milk costs four times more than it did ten years ago. Cheese was quite a lot cheaper ten years ago.

1 What could you buy for £2.50 ten years ago? What can you buy for £2.50 today?

Make your own shopping list of five things from the chart above. How much did your shopping cost ten years ago?

Which supermarket gives you the best value?

	A	B	C
Butter (250 g)	52p	44p	47p
Eggs (12)	95½p	99p	94p
Tea (125 g)	47p	55p	54p
Potatoes (kg)	25p	24p	26p
Milk (litre)	42p	39p	45p
Bread (large)	53p	54p	58p
Cheese (½ kg)	£1.20	96p	£1.35

Supermarket A's butter is the most expensive, but its tea is the cheapest. Bread from supermarket B is more expensive than bread from supermarket A, but supermarket C's is the most expensive.

2 Look at your shopping list from Exercise 1. Find out from your partner:
Where are eggs the cheapest? How much are they?

How much does your shopping cost? (From Supermarket A, B, C; buying the cheapest things in all three supermarkets.)

3 You want to buy a loaf of bread, 500 g of tea, a kilo of potatoes, a litre of milk and 100 g of cheese. Which supermarket gives you the best value?

4 Write down the names of three supermarkets in your town, and make a chart of ten items of food and their prices.

Which supermarket gives you the best value?

5 Now write about the supermarkets.
_____ is cheaper for eggs, but it's more expensive for coffee. The fruit in _____ is a lot more expensive than _____.

SUMMARY

Now you can:

use superlatives

KEY GRAMMAR
Question forms
What can you buy for £2.50?
Which supermarket is the best value?
When is the best time to call?
Which is nearer to England, Finland or Germany?
Which is the nearest, Finland, Germany or the USA?

Statements
Milk costs twice as much now as it did ten years ago.
Supermarket A's butter is the most expensive, but its tea is the cheapest.
Before midday is the most expensive time.

Vocabulary
butter
bread
cheese
milk

call
cost (cost)
phone
remember

32

People use the telephone much more these days, and we pay more and more. In the table below you can see the time difference between Britain and some other countries. You can compare the cost of telephoning from Britain to different countries. Charge Band 1 is the least expensive and Charge Band 5b is the most expensive. France is Charge Band 1 because it is the nearest country to Britain. New Zealand is the farthest country from Britain. Calls to France and Germany are quite cheap but calls to New Zealand, Australia and Hong Kong are the most expensive.

Charge bands and time differences		
	Charge band	Hours' difference from London
Australia	5b	+ 8–10
Brazil	5a	– 3
Canada	4	– 3½–9
Finland	2	+ 2
France	1	+ 1
Germany	1	+ 1
Hong Kong	5b	+ 7
New Zealand	5b	+ 12
USA (not Hawaii)	4	– 5–8

** Cheap rates 6.00 p.m.–8.00 a.m. Monday–Friday
All weekend (Saturday and Sunday)

London 12.00	Sydney 22.00	Rio de Janeiro 9.00

Toronto 06.00	Helsinki 14.00	Paris 13.00

Frankfurt 13.00	Hong Kong 19.00	Auckland 00.00

New Orleans 07.00	Singapore 19.00	Rome 13.00	Caracas 07.00

6 Look at the chart. You are in London. Ask and answer in pairs.
Which is nearer to England: Finland or Germany?
(Canada or Australia/New Zealand or the USA/Brazil or Australia)
– *Germany is nearer than Finland.*
Which is the more expensive/cheaper phone call: to Brazil or Australia? (Canada or Hong Kong/France or Finland/ New Zealand or the USA)
– *A phone call to ____ is ____ than a call to ____.*

7 You are in London. Ask and answer in pairs.
Which is the nearest/farthest: Germany, Finland or the USA?
(USA, Australia or Brazil/Canada, Hong Kong or Finland)
– *____ is the nearest/farthest.*
Which is the most expensive/cheapest phone call: to Germany, Finland or the USA?
(USA, Australia or Brazil/Canada, Hong Kong or Finland)
– *The most expensive phone call is to ____.*

8 Listen to the tape and complete the conversation.
A   Hello, operator. I'd like to call Brazil. When is the ____ time?
B   The ____ times are before ____ in the morning, after ____ at night, or at the weekends.
A   You mean it's ____ at the moment?
B   Yes, before midday is the ____ expensive time.
A   What time is it now in Sao Paulo?
B   Well, it's 11.00 a.m. here, so it's ____ there.
A   All right, I'll wait till nine tonight.
B   Yes, that's probably ____.
Now repeat the conversation, using the following:
Australia, Sydney; Germany, Munich; USA, New York.

9 Look at the following information and make dialogues in pairs like the model below.
These people live in different towns. You want to phone them next Tuesday. There is only a short time that day when they can talk on the phone. You are phoning from London: remember the difference between London time and the time in other countries. Is it better for you to phone them, or for them to phone you?

Name	Town	Call between these times
Sara	Singapore	3.00–5.00 pm
John	New Orleans	10.00 am–3.00 pm
Pekka	Helsinki	2.00–3.30 pm
Jules	Caracas	9.30–11.45 am
Coral	Hong Kong	4.00–6.30 pm
Sandra	Rome	6.00–7.15 pm

You   When is the best time to talk to you?
Sara   Between three and five in the afternoon.
You   What time is that in London?
Sara   I think it's between eight and ten in the morning.
You   That's the most expensive time! Can you call me?

32

Theme 1 Travel - learning about weather - an eccentric 65yr old man who travels around Europe

LOOKING FOR THE SUN

+ N. coast of Africa in search of sun.

2 Seasons - spring summer autumn winter

3 Intro verbs for weather simple drawings: rainy/wet sunny/dry

Phrases: have just been. one person | 2 people

4 Read silently

5 Go through text students to find past tense verbs + recent past write them down.

"It's raining/wet" "It's dry" "It's sunny" "It's windy" "It's snowing"

Robert Midhurst is 65 but he looks much younger. He has just been in Europe and North Africa on a bicycle for more than six months. Last September the weather in Britain was very bad, so Robert Midhurst got on his bicycle in London and went to Dover. It took him all day. At Dover, he took a ferry and crossed to Boulogne. After three days he reached Paris, but in Paris the weather was no better than in London. It rained all the time. Again, he got on his bike and started the journey to Perpignan, near the Spanish border.

6 Ask quest: Is R.M. younger than 65? No, he isn't.
7 What's the past tense of:
8 How do you spell it?

1 Find the past forms of these verbs from the text:
Regular: start rain cross reach
Irregular: go take get on

2. Was the weather in Brit. very bad in Sept.? Y, it was.

9 Read sentence from text in which wd appears + make a new sentence with it. Repeat for other verbs.

2 Ask and answer these questions.
Students ask
NB: "like" not in answer.

1 What was the weather like in London?
  – It/very bad.
2 What/weather/like/Paris?
  – It ____. *was bad / no better.*
3 How did he go to Dover?
  – He/by bicycle. *went*
4 How/go/Boulogne? *How did he go to B.?*
  – He ____. *went to B. by ferry.*
5 How long did it take to go from London to Dover?
  – It took ____. *all him one day.*
6 How long/take/Boulogne/Paris?
  – It ____. *took him 3 days.*

3 ans of talking about weather

Ptrn: What was the weather like?
PRESENT SIMPLE
"a) It was hot/cold/sunny/bad. but rained a lot.
There was a lot of snow
It/there used to talk about the weather today. simple present:
It's raining/ It's snowing. Present Continuous.

3 Work in groups of four. Fill in the chart. Find out:
Who has been to Paris? *← Present Perfect*
Who has been to the South of France? *✓ "ever" Have you ever been to Paris?*

Sht ans. I have/haven't

	1	2	3	4
Paris				
The South of France				
Spain				
Greece				
Rome				
The Middle East				
The USA				
North Africa				

Write about your chart:
Four people have been to ____ but nobody has been to ____.

conjunctions

Now talk about your chart with the class. In your class, where have most people been, where have only a few been?

most | A lot of people in the class have been to ____. No one has/only a few

refers to general past rather than a specific time.

Robert likes France a lot and he travelled slowly. The weather got better; the days were very sunny and warm and he often did nothing at all. He went south via Limoges and Toulouse, and it was late October when he arrived in Spain. After he crossed the border it became very cold. For five days he travelled slowly because there were strong winds, and it often rained. At the beginning of November the weather got better, and he stopped on the Costa del Sol. The sun shone but the beaches were often empty. He left Spain at the beginning of December.

Passive intro of adverbs

Test comprehension
Incorrect sentences! Students to correct them.
1 Robert doesn't like France.
2 He travelled quickly.
3 The weather got worse.
4 He did a lot.
5 He arrived in Spain in July.

Find past forms of verb.

Map labels: LONDON, ENGLAND, DOVER, BOULOGNE, ABBEVILLE, AMIENS, BEAUVAIS, PARIS, ORLEANS, BOURGES, FRANCE, LIMOGES, TOULOUSE, PERPIGNAN, BARCELONA, SPAIN, VALENCIA, ALICANTE, GRANADA, MALAGA, GIBRALTAR, COSTA DEL SOL, TANGIER, ORAN, MOROCCO, OUJDA, ALGERIA, ALGIERS, CONSTANTINE, TUNIS, TUNISIA

Practise quests weather today. What was the weather like yesterday? the day before yesterday?

33

* WKBK EXS. 1, 2 + 3.

4 Find the past forms of these verbs from the text. *put them into new sentences*
Regular   travel   arrive   stop
Irregular   shine   do   leave
       become

5 Look at the map. Robert went from Boulogne to the Costa del Sol via Paris, Limoges and Toulouse. Which other towns did he go through? Write down ten towns. Now make sentences like this:
After Limoges, he went through Toulouse.
Before Paris, he went through Beauvais. *Give me one sentence to join these pairs of towns:* (before)
before London/Dover, *before* Abbeville/Amiens,

In Morocco and Algeria he took the coast road. It was his first time in Africa and the journey was very interesting. Then he became ill in Oran and was in bed for more than a week. He ate nothing, and he nearly came back to England by plane. But he got better and the next week he left for Algiers and Tunis.

Did R. like Africa? Y. Why was he in bed in Oran? - ill. What did he eat? Nothing.

6 Find the past forms of these verbs:
Irregular   come   eat
     came   ate

7 Where was Robert in September? (October, November, December) *Morocco Spain   Costa del Sol*
How long did it take him to get from London to Boulogne? (Boulogne to Perpignan, Perpignan to the Costa del Sol, London to the Costa del Sol. *2 mths + 5days.*
France   *1 day*   *5 days.*

8 What does Robert like about Britain? Listen to the tape and look at the list below. Put a tick (√) or a cross (x).
① — *Ask students Do you like! in Britain? here?*

Does Robert like ...?	
the countryside	*② students ask the does. each other around class*
the food	N (boring)
the hotels	N - (very expensive)
the people	Y - (v. friendly)
the television	Y.
the weather	N - (hates it)
the summer	Y
the winter	N

9 Complete these sentences from the tape. *LISTENING TAPE.* *before*
1 *the Spring* is often wet.
2 In the *winter* we don't have *snow.*
3 In the winter it's *not very cold it rains a lot.*
4 The summer is *often quite good.*

Valencia/Alicante, Granada/Malaga.

10 Make sentences from this chart. Which season of the year do you like best/least?

11. What did he eat? Nothing.

Students write 4/5 sentences about likes/dislikes.

I	like don't like	summer autumn winter spring	because	it the weather	is isn't	wet. too hot. very hot. warm. too cold. very warm. very good.
				there's a lot of wind.		
				it rains a lot.		

Check ans. + ask "Which season do you like? Why?"

WKBK Exs. 4, 5, 6.

33

Have you ever been conned?

Ask! How Mr Barratt asks if the man's in trouble.

con   verb, to con
someone. Take
money, but give
nothing back.
Lie, cheat.

conman   man taking money
from others.

This man looks like a doctor, but he isn't a Dr. He's a conman.

34

Read silently:

Some people can always make money. This
man, for example, looks like a businessman, or
a doctor, but he isn't; he's a conman. He's quite
famous, and he has got a lot of money.
How does he do it? Here's an example.
(Last week) Ian Barratt was out with his dog,
when he met an old man. The old man was
about sixty, with white hair and blue eyes. He
also had a moustache and a beard. His suit
looked very expensive and he carried a small
case.

Ans: TRUE/False. If false students to correct.

1) This man is a businessman. F / Mr Barratt met an old man last wk. T
2) He looks like a conman. F / 3) The old man looked very smart. T
3) He hasn't got any money. F

---

2) Students introduced passively to direct object pronouns.

1 Find the past forms of these verbs from the text:
Regular   carry   look   *1) write them down.*
Irregular   have   meet   *2) Spell the past forms*
   3) what else in text tells us it's in   *3) Read the sentences they come from*
   the past — (Last week)   *4) Make new sentences with past forms*

2 Listen to the tape. Mr Barratt is talking to the old
man. Are these sentences true or false? *correct false ones.*

F.   1   Mr Barratt knows the other man. *he doesn't.*

T.   2   The other man is (in trouble.) = *something isn't right.*

F.   3   Mr Barratt wants to get a taxi. *The other man wants a taxi.*

F.   4   The old man gives Mr Barratt some money.
   He asks for some money.

   story is unfinished.

3 Complete the story. Choose three of these sentences. *i*
Mr Barratt didn't lend the old man anything.   *one from*
✻Mr Barratt lent the old man ten pounds.   *each pair.*
Mr Barratt didn't give the old man his address.
✻Mr Barratt gave the old man his address.   *(check students*
The old man returned the money.   *use pronouns)*
✻The old man didn't return the money.

2 students to summarise the whole story,
finishing with their sentences.

4 You want to get some money. Here is a list
of things: *Intro. indirect obj. with LEND.*
Ptn! Can you lend me some money? ✻ *Most likely ending.*
sweater   pair of shoes   camera   newspaper
bar of chocolate   watch   bunch of flowers
Copy substitution table? T.B
Choose one or more, write the prices down on a piece of
paper and ask your partner for the money. *e.g. newspaper/25p.*

A   Can you lend me some money?
B   Why do you want it? *(newspaper)*
A   I want to buy a _____ *(newspaper)*
B   Oh, all right. Is ___ *(25p)* enough?
A   Er ... well ... can you lend me ___ *(50p)* ?
B   { Yes, here's ___ *(50p)*
   { I'm afraid I can't. Here's ___ *20p*.
A   Thanks very much.
B   When will you return it? *Wk6b*
A   I'll give it back on *Wed.*   *Ex 145.*

Bdwk. I'll return it to you tomorrow
introducing future simple tense.

Have you ever seen an advertisement like this? It's
another example of a con.

ASK! what else did you put at end of sentence? nxt wk/ yr/mth.

Bdwk: I'll lend you some money. when will you return it?

Substitution table:

Can you	lend	me	a story?
	give	us	your book.
	show	him	a car?
	tell	her	some money.
		them	your pen?
			your address

When this appeared in the newspaper over a thousand
people answered and sent £10. They were very unhappy
with the information they got and called the police, but
when the police went to the address it was too late.
There was no-one there. The woman next door told
them: "Two men lived there, one was tall, and very good-
looking. The other was quite short and fat. Last week
they bought a new car and left."

Why was everybody unhappy? Because in return for their ten pounds the conmen sent them this short note:

> Dear Friend,
> Thank you for your money. You too can make a lot of money. Simply put an advertisement like this in the newspaper:
> Do you want to make a lot of money?
> Send £10 for more information.
> Thank you very much. Good luck!

5 Find the past forms of these verbs from the text:
Regular   answer   live   call   appear
Irregular   send   tell   leave   buy

6 Make sentences from this chart.

Give	John the policeman Hans and Wolf Pierre and me Martine your neighbour	the some	money. ticket. information. address. fruit. telephone number.

Now change the sentences, like this:
Give John the money. = Give it to him.
(Use *it*, *him*, *her*, *them*, *us*)

7 Look at the pictures of these four people.
Describe each one of them, like the model.
Use the underlined words.

A<u>'s got</u> short, dark hair and brown eyes. He's quite tall. He's <u>wearing</u> dark trousers and a blue shirt, he's wearing glasses and he's carrying a small case. He <u>looks like</u> a doctor.

8 The police are looking for **A** above. This is the form describing him:

> Hair: DARK, SHORT   Eyes: BROWN
> Height: 1.75 M
> Clothes: DARK TROUSERS, BLUE SHIRT

The police are looking for your next-door neighbour.
Make a police form for him/her.
Now tell the police about him/her.
____ lives in the house to the right. ____ is a ____ and has ____ hair and ____ eyes. He/she is ____ and quite ____. He/she is ____ and has ____ child/children.

9 Your neighbour's young daughter has not come home. Write about her for the police. Use these words:
She is ____.
She has ____.
She is wearing ____.

Verbs: return
adj. good looking
phrases: in trouble
nouns: information, neighbour, moustache, next door

34

A

B

C

D

FEAR OF FLYING

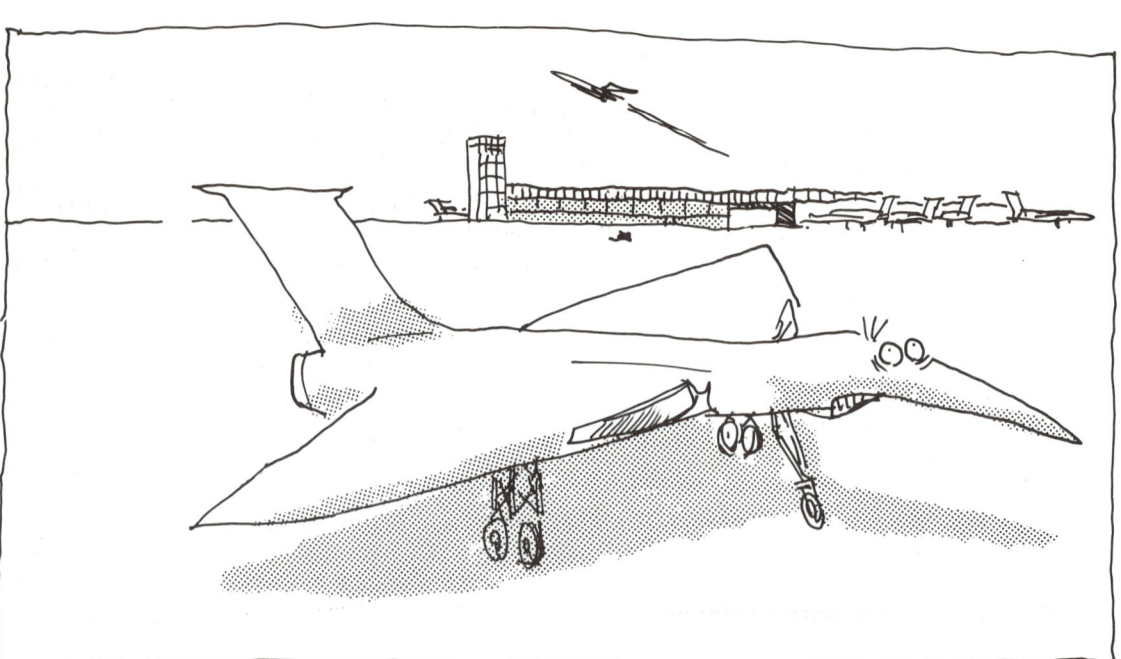

People are afraid of different things. Some people are afraid of flying; before a flight they worry for days. Some people prefer a two-day train journey, when the plane journey takes only two hours. Other people take pills, or drink a lot before the journey. The same people are usually completely unafraid of cars, trains, bicycles, ships or buses. But, in fact, some of these are much more dangerous. Look at this chart.

train	* * *
car	* * * * * *
ship	* *
plane	*

* = safest

1 Compare the dangers of travelling. Complete these sentences:
1 Flying is ____ dangerous ____ travelling by ship.

2 Driving is ____ dangerous ____ train travel.
3 Flying is the ____ dangerous way of travelling.
4 The most dangerous way of travelling is ____ .
5 There are ____ accidents with trains than with ____ every year.

Fear of flying is a phobia. Are you afraid of flying? Do you have any phobias at all? Here are the names of some common phobias:
claustrophobia – fear of crowds and small spaces
agoraphobia – fear of open spaces
vertigo – fear of heights

2 Listen to the tape. Match the phobias (1, 2 and 3) with cartoons **A**, **B** and **C** below and name them.
Phobia 1 is ____ Cartoon ____
Phobia 2 is ____ Cartoon ____
Phobia 3 is ____ Cartoon ____

3 Listen to the tape again. Find the past forms of these verbs:

Regular	walk
Irregular	go up
	feel
	get in/out
	can
	sit

4 People can be afraid of lots of other things. Here are some examples:

the dark	*being alone*
water	*crowds*
exams	*fire*
the telephone	*meeting new people*

Ask and answer questions like this:
Are you afraid of exams?
– Yes, I am./No, I'm not.
Have you got agoraphobia?
– {Yes, I'm afraid of / No, I'm not afraid of} open spaces.

A

B

C

5 Complete the sentences below. What is the speaker afraid of? Write the answers. Use the phobias from Exercises 2 and 4.

1 He lives with some friends because ____ .
2 He doesn't want to climb the Eiffel Tower because ____ .
3 She doesn't like going to parties because ____ .
4 She always travels by ship or train because ____ .
5 She can't leave the house because ____ .
6 He always writes letters to his friends because ____ .
7 She always sleeps with a light on because ____ .
8 He doesn't like swimming because ____ .

6 What can you do if you're afraid of something? Work in groups of three, Person A chooses a phobia from Exercise 4 and the others think of some good advice, like this:
I'm afraid of the dark. What can I do?
– *You can sleep with the light on.*
– *You can take sleeping pills.*
– *You can go to the doctor.*

7 Listen to the tape. A woman is visiting her doctor. Why? What's wrong with her? What does the doctor tell her? He tells her:
Go ____ , then ____ . I'll give you ____ , take ____ . Come back ____ .

8 Work in pairs. Look at the lists below. Which advice can you give for each problem?

What's the best thing for a . . .

headache?	Take some
backache?	medicine.
earache?	Rest in bed.
toothache?	Don't go to work.
stomach ache?	Don't eat anything.
	Don't drink any
	alcohol.
	Go to a party.
	Don't eat any
	sweets.
	Drink a little
	brandy.
	Rest in a dark
	room.
	Go to the dentist.

Many people are also frightened of animals; some have real phobias. Some people are frightened of snakes, others are frightened of mice. Quite a lot of people hate spiders, others have a phobia about dogs.

9 Look at the animals in the chart below.
Ask and answer in pairs.
Are you frightened of mice? (frogs, dogs, spiders . . .)
– *Yes, I am./No, I'm not.*
Which animal are you most afraid of?
– *I'm most afraid of ____ .*

10 Group survey
Who is frightened of mice in your class? Fill in the chart below. Now write about the fears of your class. Use these words:
____ is/are afraid of ____ .
____ is/are frightened of ____ .
____ doesn't/does like ____ .

mice	dogs
People afraid	
snakes	bulls
People afraid	
spiders	frogs
People afraid	
bats	cockroaches
People afraid	

REVISION

1 Letter-writing

You want to go to Britain by car. Write a letter to the AA in London. Ask for information about:

times of ferries
cost of ferries
insurance
maps
hotels

Dear Carrie

I want to take my family to Europe next month, by car. How can I get some information? For example, do I need an international driving licence? How do I get insurance? Where can I get information about prices of ferries?
Yours sincerely Martin

Dear Martin
Write to the AA (Automobile Association) in London. You can find their address in a telephone directory.
For some countries in Europe you can use a British driving licence. In Germany, for example, you don't need an international driving licence. There are a lot of ferries, and a lot of different shipping companies. I am sending the names, addresses and telephone numbers of some of the bigger ones.
Carrie

2 Comparing weights

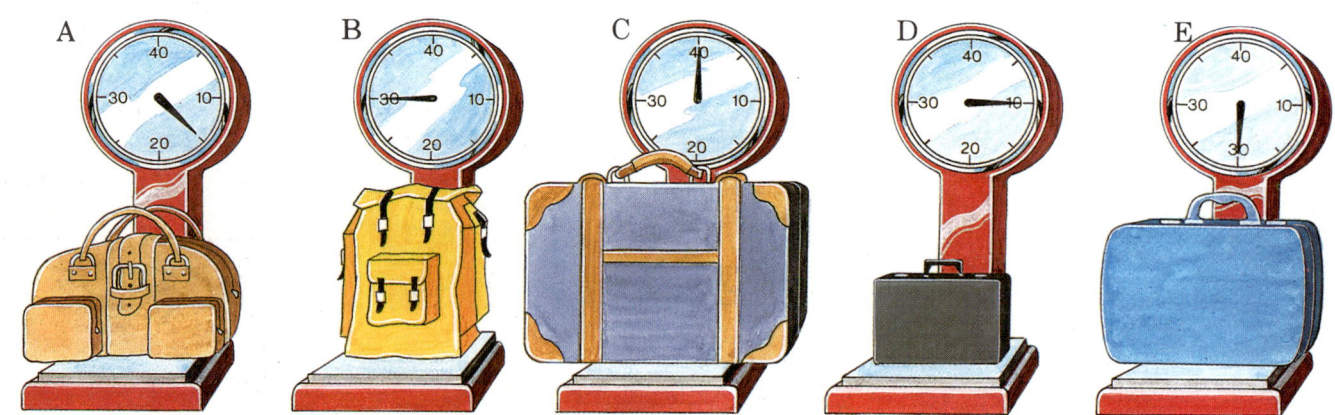

Make sentences like this:
A is smaller/lighter than C. D. is the lightest case.

3 Quiz

Match columns **A** and **B**.

A	B
What do you feel like when:	
you have no sleep	hot
you have no water	cold
you have no friends	afraid
you have no food	happy
the temperature is 35°C	sad
the temperature is 1°C	tired
you see a snake	lonely
you leave your family	thirsty
you have a holiday	hungry

4 The weather today

	Yesterday's weather		Today's weather	
London	C	10°	R	12°
Rome	S	28°	C	27°
Paris	R	18°	S	21°
Bergen	S	16°	S	20°
	C = cloud	S = sun	R = rain	

Make sentences like this:
In London today it is rainy and quite cold. (sunny, cloudy)
Yesterday it was cold and cloudy in London, but in Paris it rained.

Now talk about today's and yesterday's weather in your town.

5 Temperature charts

	Jan	Feb	March	April	May	June	July	Aug	Sep	Oct	Nov	Dec
London	4	5	7	9	12	16	18	17	15	11	8	5
Rome	8	9	11	14	18	22	25	25	22	17	13	10
Lisbon	11	12	14	16	17	20	22	23	21	18	14	12
Singapore	26	27	28	28	28	28	28	27	27	27	27	27
Rio de Janeiro	26	26	25	24	22	21	21	21	21	22	23	25

° Centigrade

Ask and answer: *When is the best time to visit Rome?*
The best time to visit Rome is in ____.

6 The best way to travel

Which travels slowly? Which travels quickly?

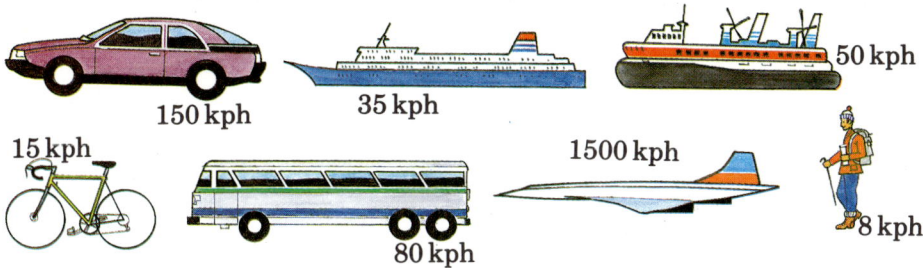

150 kph   35 kph   50 kph   15 kph   1500 kph   80 kph   8 kph

Make sentences like this:
You can travel very/quite/quickly by ____ but you can only travel very slowly by ____.

7

Here are some verbs from Units 31 to 35. What are they?

W_RR_   BR__K

SH_NE   _SE   F_LL

B_IL   PO_R   ST_R

PR_FE_   C_VER

8

Find the names of frightening animals:
Eg SOEMU = mouse

DRSIPE
SOEMU
ODG
KEANS
GORF
RCKCACOOH
ATB   LLBU

36

9 Crossword

Complete the crossword with words from Units 31–35.

ACROSS

1 A fear of something.
4 The boat from France to England.
6 A ____ of open spaces is called agoraphobia.
7 What's the best ____ for butter?
9 The plane is flying ____ the mountains.
11 Knowledge about something.
13 Ill.
17 Things you need to make something.
19 You make tea in a ____.

DOWN

2 The Vosges are the ____ between France and Germany.
3 Use to tell people about something.
4 Past of *feel*.
5 Fear of heights.
8 Opposite of *most*.
10 To take money from someone.
12 What's your telephone ____?
14 We use it to boil water in.
15 We drink tea or coffee from this.
16 To mix sugar in tea we ____ it with a spoon.
18 Past of *meet*.

A year in the life of . . .

Next week John Bennett, a London publishing company, will publish a new book. The author is now dead, but he wrote the book when he was only twelve years old. It's his diary from the year 1903. In that year the author, James Houseman, was away from home, living at school. What was life like in an English school in the early years of this century? This diary gives us a lot of information about it. Here, for example, is one page, from Friday, June 12th, 1903.

1 Match these questions and answers.

Who wrote the diary?	He or she writes books.
Who will publish the diary?	James Houseman did.
How old was the author?	It was Friday, June 12th.
What was the date?	John Bennett will.
What does an author do?	He was twelve.

2 Say three things you will do next week.
Use these verbs:

see   go to   buy   meet   phone

> FRIDAY   12 JUNE 1903
>
> I woke up very early today, before six o'clock. The nineteen other boys were still asleep, but I couldn't go back to sleep because it was so cold. There was ice in the wash basins. I went to the window and looked out; it was still dark and there was snow on the ground.
> For breakfast we had hot cereal, egg, sausages, mushrooms and tomatoes. I hate hot cereal, but I had to eat it. After breakfast I felt very sick. I went to the nurse and she put her hand on my head. "There's nothing wrong with you, Houseman," she said. "Go and have a cold bath."
> I'm going to tell my father about the nurse.

3 Find the past forms of these verbs from the page above:

Regular	look out
Irregular	feel
	have to
	say
	wake up
	put

4 Work in pairs. Ask questions, about James first, then about your partner.
What did James have for breakfast that morning?
– He had hot cereal, eggs, sausages, mushrooms and tomatoes.
What did you have for breakfast this morning?

5 Find the past forms of these verbs from the page on the left:

Regular	play
	kick
Irregular	put
	fall
	smell

> In the morning there was a French lesson. I don't like French because I can't understand it. Old McVicar, the teacher, is from Scotland. He's never been to France. I felt very tired in McVicar's lesson and I went to sleep. In the afternoon we played football. I don't like football. Another boy kicked me and I fell down. McVicar looked at me and said, "There's nothing wrong with you, boy. Get up and run round the field five times." I'm going to tell my father about McVicar. Dinner today was horrible and I wasn't hungry: the potatoes were cold, the meat was very tough and it smelt bad. I couldn't eat the meat so I put it on the floor for the mice. Tomorrow is Saturday. Maybe it will be better than today because my father is going to bring my sister here and perhaps we'll go to London for lunch. I'm going to eat a lot tomorrow! I'm also going to tell my father about McVicar and the nurse! Now it's time to go to sleep. It's cold in this room but I feel very tired tonight.

6 Make sentences from both texts. Match the questions to the answers.

Why	did didn't	he	wake up early? feel sick? go to the nurse? go to sleep in the French lesson? fall down? eat his dinner? put the meat on the floor?

Because	a boy he it	felt very tired. smelt very bad. ate hot cereal. couldn't eat it. kicked him hard. was very cold. felt sick.

7 Do you know the second meaning of the word 'diary'? It is also a book for notes of appointments and meetings, like the one below.

MONDAY	
TUESDAY	8.30 go to Alan's
WEDNESDAY	7.00 children's school concert
THURSDAY	
FRIDAY	6.30 meet Anna for dinner 9.30 disco
SATURDAY	8.00 Lucio's Restaurant
SUNDAY	Tidy flat 6.00 visit mother

Make a diary for next week. Write an activity (or two) for the evening of five days (like the diary above). Now make dialogues with your partner. Find a free evening.

A I'm going to the theatre on Monday evening. Do you want to come?

B { No, I'm going to watch a film on television and then/ after that I'm going to bed early.
Yes, I'm free on Monday evening. I'd love to.

8 Ask and answer in pairs.
1 What day is it today?
2 What's the date?
3 What is the day after tomorrow?
4 What was the day before yesterday?
5 When's your birthday?
6 When's the next public holiday?

9 Complete a diary for today or yesterday.
Today/yesterday I woke up at ____ .
The weather ____ .
For breakfast I ____ .
After breakfast I ____ .
Then I ____ .
For lunch ____ .
After lunch ____ .
Then ____ .
Tomorrow I ____ .

10 Listen to the tape and complete the sentences below. The interviewer is talking to James Houseman's grandson.
James Houseman's grandson is also called ____ . He is at the ____ as his ____ . The school is the same as in the diary. The bedrooms are the same because ____ and the rooms are ____ . Breakfast is almost the same; the boys now eat ____ , then they have ____ and finally they have ____ .

37

SUMMARY

Now you can :

talk about your plans
talk about the date

KEY GRAMMAR
Question forms
What's the date? It's January 3rd.

Future forms
I'm going to tell my father.
John Bennett will publish the book.
The day after tomorrow is Thursday.

Vocabulary
fall down (fell)
kick
listen
publish
study
wake up (woke up)
watch

Eating Greek in London

Takis Aristopoulos, the famous restaurateur, has just opened a new restaurant in London. His restaurants in Athens and Paris are already very famous. Takis is a quiet man, but an excellent chef. A friend of his once told me: 'Takis doesn't need to talk, his food says everything.' And he was right!

I went to Takis' on the opening night. I took three friends – Gerd from Berlin, and Patrice and Claire. Gerd doesn't often eat Greek food, but Patrice and Claire lived in Athens five years ago and they know a lot about it. Their favourite food is Greek.

1 Answer these questions.
Have you eaten Greek food?
Do you like it?
What do you like?
What's your favourite food?

2 Fill in the chart.

	I lived in	I worked in
1 year ago		
5 years ago		
10 years ago		
15 years ago		
20 years ago		

Now ask and answer in pairs.
A year ago I lived in Paris. Where did you live?
– I lived in _____.
Where did you work?
Where were you five years ago?

The food was excellent. First we all had salads: Gerd had a tomato salad and I had a green salad. Gerd's salad was better than mine. Claire and Patrice both had yoghurt salad. Theirs was very good.

Next Patrice had kleftiko and I had afelia. They were both under five pounds. Gerd and Claire had fish; he had sole and she had prawns. The sole was six pounds, the prawns seven.

Our meat was excellent, and their fish was very good too. We all had fruit dishes for dessert. Gerd and I had melon in pastry with cream. The others had peaches in honey. Ours was lovely, but theirs was very sweet.

The evening at Takis' was wonderful – the wine was excellent, the service good and the food not too expensive. We're all going to go back soon.

SUSAN GRANGER

Takis

STARTERS

TARAMASALATA – smoked cod roe with oil and lemon juice	£0.95
HOUMOUS – chick peas with olive oil and lemon juice	£0.95
MELON	£1.10
YOGHURT SALAD	£0.70

SALADS

GREEN SALAD	£0.65
TOMATO SALAD	£0.75
MIXED SALAD	£0.70

MAIN COURSES
served with rice and salad

DONER KEBAB – tender sliced lamb	£3.25
LAMB KEBAB – cubes of tender lamb with onions and peppers	£3.50
KLEFTIKO – roast leg of lamb	£3.85
AFELIA – pork in wine	£3.50
STIFADO – beef in red wine	£5.25
YOGHURT KEBAB – lamb in yoghurt and tomato sauce	£3.75
SOLE	£6.00
PRAWN SALAD	£7.00
KALAMARES – fried squid	£5.50

DESSERTS

MELON PASTRY	£1.25
PEACHES IN HONEY	£1.15
ICE-CREAM	£0.95
FRUIT SALAD	£0.95

DRINKS

	bottle	glass
RED WINE	£4.50	£0.80
WHITE WINE	£4.50	£0.80
COFFEE	£0.45	

3 Make sentences, like this:
Patrice – yoghurt salad/Susan – green salad – good
Patrice had a yoghurt salad and Susan had a green salad. Hers was good but his was better.
1 Susan – green salad/Patrice – yoghurt salad – good
2 Gerd – fish/Susan – afelia – cheap
3 Gerd – fish/Susan and Patrice – meat – good
4 Gerd – melon/Claire – peaches – sweet

4 Make sentences like this:

		Italian French English Chinese Indian Greek	restaurants because the	food meat waiters salads desserts drinks	are is	sweeter better cheaper hotter stronger more interesting	than ours.
I	like don't like						

Then add a second sentence:
But I think our ____ is/are ____ than theirs.

5 Listen to the tape. Write down what the man and woman are going to eat.

6 Listen to the tape again. Now work in groups of three.
Two of you are eating at Takis'. The third is the waiter/waitress.
Make a dialogue like the one on tape, using the information below.

CUSTOMERS

You want:
Starter – **A** taramasalata
            B melon
Main course – **A** stifado
                B kebab
Dessert – Fruit salad

WAITER
Take the customers' order. In the restaurant today you haven't got any melon or stifado.

7 Four people ate at Takis'. These are the meals:

Valentin	*Rosemarie*	*Lucio*	*Christa*
tomato salad	*taramasalata*	*tomato salad*	*houmous*
lamb kebab	*prawn salad*	*squid*	*tomato salad*
ice cream	*melon*	*peaches*	*water*
coffee	*coffee*	*coffee*	
2 glasses red wine	*1 glass white wine*	*4 glasses white wine*	

Write the answers to these questions:
1 How much did Valentin pay for his meal?
2 Who paid the most?
3 Who paid the least?
4 Did Christa have any meat?
5 Did Rosemarie have any meat?
6 Who had the most wine?
7 Who didn't have any coffee?

8 Look at the passages again. Choose one of the characters from
Exercise 7. Now you write about Takis', starting like this:
I went to Takis' with three friends, ____, ____ and ____. ____ is from and
____ and ____ are from ____. I had ____ to start and ____ had ____. They
were both very good...

38

AWAY FROM IT ALL

Many holiday towns on the Mediterranean are crowded. Sometimes you can't even find a place on the beach. Often, the food is not very good. But there are still some very good places. Here, for example, are three Mediterranean towns, all quite small, but then the largest holiday towns are often not the best.

1 Read the three passages, then make sentences, like this:

swim – waterski
When I last went on holiday, I swam but I couldn't waterski.

sunbathe – swim
eat fish – eat prawns
go sightseeing – take boat trips
drink wine – drink brandy

2 Make true sentences.

My	house flat car English room work life friends	is are	very quite not very	good. large. small. easy. difficult. nice.

Now ask your partner:

I'm	quite not very very	tired, hungry, thirsty, bored,	are you?

3 Ask and answer in pairs.
I can't swim very well, can you? (ski, waterski, windsurf, do yoga, play tennis, ...)
– Yes, I can./No, I can't.

Have you been to Cresta yet?

Not far from Barcelona, Cresta is a busy town with narrow streets and interesting shops. All the family can swim safely in the sea or sunbathe on the wide, sandy beach. Stay at the Bay or Esplanada Hotels and you can take a boat to the many little resorts in the area. You'll find the Dolphin and the Castle restaurants very pleasant, with cheap but good food at the first. At the Castle you'll have to pay a little more, but you'll love the seafood, fresh from the Mediterranean.

The Smiths have already been to Thera several times – and this year they're going again.

This is only a small village, with a small beach. You won't find any large and expensive hotels, but small and friendly pensions with good simple food. On Thera you can swim, waterski, windsurf and do any other sport you can think of.

One day take the road from the village up to the hill. Be careful of it; it's narrow and very steep, but the view from the top is amazing. Thera has already become quite popular, but in early and late summer the hotels are not very full. Book now!

St Theresa isn't very crowded yet, but in a few years it will be. Go now!

St Theresa is only a few kilometres from Naples. It's quite small, with very good nightlife, and a lot of good clean hotels. You can eat cheaply and the food is excellent – one of the best restaurants is Toni's – the fish is very fresh – you choose your fish from a large tank. It's best to go early or late, in May or September. There are quite a few visitors in the middle of summer, but St Theresa isn't as crowded yet as the larger resorts.

4 Ask and answer in pairs.
Would you like to go to Greece next summer? (Morocco, Scandinavia, Ireland . . .)
– No, I've already been there./Yes, perhaps. I haven't been there yet.

5 Listen to the tape and answer these questions.
Where are the women going on holiday?
When?
What's good about Spain?
Why didn't one woman go there last year?

Now make dialogues, like this, with your partner:
Where are you going next ____?
– I don't know yet.
Let's go to ____.
– That's a good idea./Oh, I've already been there. Let's go to ____.

6 Talk about your home town. Tell your class about it.
When you come to ____, you must eat at (drink at, visit, see, go to) the ____. You'll love the ____. When you come to ____, don't ____ because ____.

7 Name things in the text that are:
narrow   steep   wide
simple   busy   popular
Use these words to describe your home town.

8 Do you know any holiday towns? Write about one, like the texts on the left and above. Say what you can and can't do, and what it is good to do.

9 Make one or two warnings for each of these places, like this:

the zoo – be careful of the animals

the zoo
a busy town
a modern kitchen
a beach
the sea

10 Listen to the tape and complete the table.
A tourist is talking to someone in the tourist information office. She wants to find a good hotel and she has started this table.

	SWIMMING POOL	BEACH	RESTAURANT	TELEPHONE NUMBER	COST PER NIGHT
BEAUREGARD	✓	✓	excellent	✓	£50+
FOUR SEASONS					
WINTER GARDEN					
SUMMER PALACE					
STELLA MARIS					

Which hotel does she choose?

SUMMARY

Now you can:

talk about things you've already done, and things you haven't done yet

KEY GRAMMAR
Question forms
Have you been to Cresta yet?
Would you like to go to Greece?

Short forms
Yes, I can.
No, I can't.

General statements
I've already been to Cresta.
I haven't been to Cresta yet.
I swam but I couldn't waterski.
You'll love the food, you must eat the seafood.

Adverbs
cheaply
safely
well

Vocabulary
be careful of   busy
go sightseeing   crowded
sunbathe   narrow
visit   popular
waterski   simple
windsurf   steep
                     wide
beach
resort
view

39

83

40

1 Match the book titles above with these descriptions.
Fill in the gaps with the name of the book.

1 You've never been to China? You don't have to go there to eat the food, at least. With this book you can learn to cook Chinese food cheaply and easily. ____ will make a lovely Christmas present for one of your friends.

2 The author of this new mystery is B.G. Fourbanks. Who is ____? Read the book and find out, but be careful, it's very frightening!

3 Where is it? What is the population? What are the names of the towns and rivers? ____ tells you, with every map in full colour.

4 What will life be like in the future? No-one knows, of course, but ____ is about a family over 1,000 years from now. Read this exciting new science fiction story.

5 ____ is a romance about a beautiful young woman. She falls in love with a soldier but he has to go to war. Will she ever see him again?

6 ____ describes hotels, restaurants, shops and beaches in most European countries. Buy this book and you'll get *Holidays in Britain* free.

7 Do you like adventure stories? This one is very exciting. ____ is about a diver in South America. You won't be able to put it down.

8 She was beautiful. She came from Austria and lived and died in France. This historical novel is about the colourful life with the French royal family before the French Revolution.

9 Have you read this one yet? ____ is an important book for business people, housewives and retired people. Anyone can make money with this book.

10 *The Book of Sports 1* tells you about more than fifty different European sports. Have you read it? Then you must read ____; it will tell you about more than 200 sports around the world.

BOOKS BOOKS

2 Make a list of four books from your country.
Ask and answer in pairs.
Have you read ___ yet?
– Yes, I have./No, I haven't.
Now recommend books to your partner.
Read ___ . You'll like it, I did.
– { *I've already read it. I like it too./I didn't like it.*
  { *I haven't read that one yet. Who's the author?*

3 Write about a book.
Last year I read ___ . It's a/an historical novel (science fiction, mystery, romance, adventure story).
It's by ___ .
It's about ___ .
I liked it/didn't like it. It's a very long/exciting/interesting/boring/difficult/sad book.

4 Listen to the tape and answer the questions.
The name of the first book is ___ .
The author is ___ .
The woman has already finished a book by ___ .
The man doesn't like ___ .
The second book is called a) 2001 b) 2010 c) 2002
It's a) a romance b) an adventure story
   c) a science fiction story
It's by a) Arthur Clarke b) Heywood Floyd
   c) HAL 9000
It's very a) funny b) frightening c) exciting

5 Ask and answer in pairs. Fill in the chart with information about your partner: (Write a tick ✓)

Do you like fiction or non-fiction?
Which kind of fiction do you like best?
Which kind of non-fiction do you like best?

Non-fiction		Fiction	
Travel	☐	Mystery	☐
Sport	☐	Science Fiction	☐
Food	☐	Romance	☐
Money	☐	Adventure	☐
		Historical novel	☐

Now choose one or two books for your partner and complete the order form.

Name ....
Address ....
....
Telephone .... (day) .... (evening)
Name of books ....
....
Catalogue nos ....
Price ....
Send to Bodick & Crawley PO Box 787 London SE1

6 Write sentences about your partner and yourself.
___ likes ___ books, and I like ___ . He/she likes ___ in particular, but I like ___ . I'm going to buy ___ and ___ going to buy ___ .

7 Listen to the questions from the tape.
Write each question next to the word it asks/tells about, like the example.

Title *(What are you reading now?)*
Author
Type of book
Description of story
Reasons for liking/not liking it

Now ask your partner about a book, using the questions above.

40

SUMMARY

Now you can:

talk about books

KEY GRAMMAR
Question forms
Do you like fiction or non-fiction?
Which kind of fiction do you like best?
Who's it by?
What's it about?

General statements
This novel is about . . .
It's a very exciting book.
It's by . . .

Adverbs
cheaply
easily

Vocabulary
fiction/non-fiction   mystery
adventure   romance
historical novel   science fiction novel

HANNIBAL
THE FILM

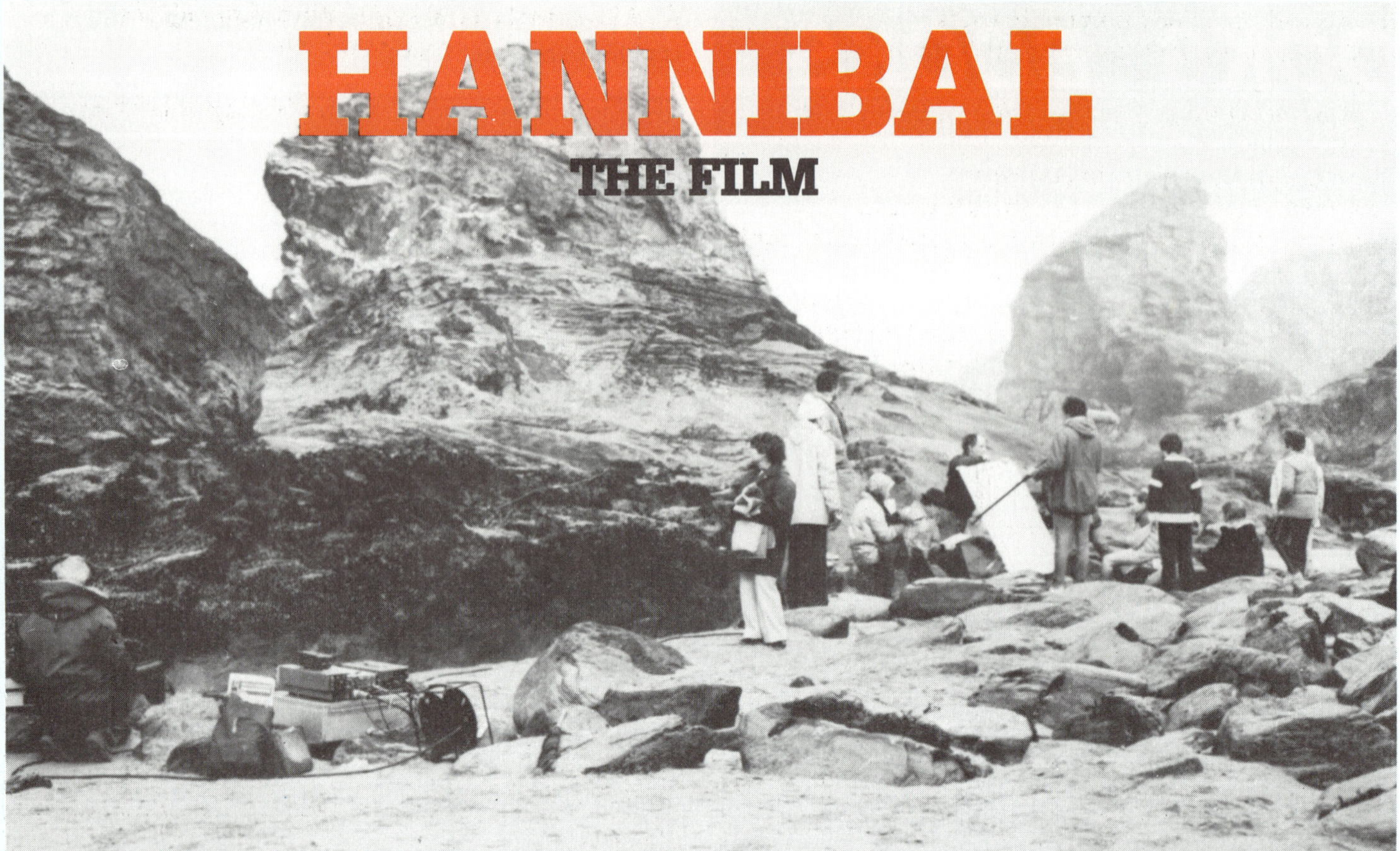

Director: George Castle Film: Hannibal Type: Adventure/history Setting: Spain/North Africa
Stars: Robert West/Inge Johannsen

Global studios are spending nearly £30,000,000 on their latest film *Hannibal*. The story takes place in North Africa and the Pyrenees.

There are many famous stars in this film. Robert West, in his fiftieth film, is earning £3,000,000. George Castle, the director, arrived in Spain two months ago, and they're filming now. They'll go to North Africa next month and do some more filming.

You can see Hannibal in London, New York and Paris in April next year.

1 Listen to the sentences on the tape. Are they true or false?

2 Look at the set and listen to the tape.
The director is giving instructions to the actors, he's telling them to stand in the right place for the next scene. Which actors are **A**, **B**, **C**, **D** and **E**.

Actors: Robert West, Inge Johannsen, Jennifer Steadman, Louis Ranulph, Roy Keane.

3 Talk about entertainment in pairs.
How often do you go to the cinema? (the theatre, a restaurant, a concert . . .)
– I go to the cinema once (twice, three times) a week (month, year).
When did you last go to the cinema?
– I went to the cinema ____ weeks ago/on ____ .
How many times have you been to the cinema this year?

4 Group survey
Global Studios are spending nearly £30,000,000 on the film, but is it worth it? Do people go to the cinema very often today?
Fill in the chart in groups of four, using these questions:
How often do you go to the cinema now?
How often did you go to the cinema five years ago?

	Now	Five years ago
A		
B		
C		
D		

once a year = almost never
2–5 times a year = rarely
6–20 times a year = quite often
21–40 times a year = often
41–60 times a year = very often

5 Ask around the class:
Do you/does ____ (name) often go to the cinema?
– Yes, I do./No, he doesn't.
How often?
– Quite often, about 15 times a year.

6 Write a summary about your group.
In this group ____ people go to the cinema quite often and ____ . Five years ago ____ . In this group people go to the cinema more/less often than ____ .

7 Listen to the tape again. Write down all the prepositions you hear, for example:
from, by, next to . . .
Now discuss places in your town in pairs, like this:
Where's the nearest post office?
– It's near the station.

8 Copy the map from Exercise 2.
Now add: a tree, another soldier, a road, a bridge over the stream and a small house.
Work in pairs. A asks: *'Where's your road?' (tree, soldier, bridge, house)*. B answers: *'It's near the ____ .'* and A draws it. Now look at your maps. Are they the same?

9 Fill in the table below. Choose your favourite film and two films that are in cinemas in your town now.

	1	2	3
Title			
Name of star(s)			
Name of director			
Length of film			
Place of story			
Type of film (adventure, romance etc)			

10 Write about your favourite film.
Use the information above and the following questions.
Where did you see it?
When did you see it?
Why did you like it?

41

SUMMARY

Now you can :

talk about films
talk about position

KEY GRAMMAR
Question forms
How often do you go to the cinema?
Where's the nearest cinema?

General statements
I rarely go to the cinema.
She doesn't go to the cinema very often.
It's near the station.

Prepositions
behind
between
by
from
in front of
next to

Vocabulary
film
spend (spent)
take place
actor/actress
director

entertainment
favourite
scene
set

REVISION

1 Letter-writing

Write a letter to a friend in Britain and tell him/her about traffic rules in your country.
Use these ideas:
Speed limits in towns and on motorways
Left or right side of the road
Lights on your car (colour, when you use them)
Driving and alcohol

CALENDAR FOR 1985

	JANUARY					FEBRUARY					MARCH				
MONDAY		7	14	21	28		4	11	18	25		4	11	18	25
TUESDAY	1	8	15	22	29		5	12	19	26		5	12	19	26
WEDNESDAY	2	9	16	23	30		6	13	20	27		6	13	20	27
THURSDAY	3	10	17	24	31		7	14	21	28		7	14	21	28
FRIDAY	4	11	18	25		1	8	15	22		1	8	15	22	29
SATURDAY	5	12	19	26		2	9	16	23		2	9	16	23	30
SUNDAY	6	13	20	27		3	10	17	24		3	10	17	24	31

	APRIL					MAY					JUNE				
MONDAY	1	8	15	22	29		6	13	20	27		3	10	17	24
TUESDAY	2	9	16	23	30		7	14	21	28		4	11	18	25
WEDNESDAY	3	10	17	24		1	8	15	22	29		5	12	19	26
THURSDAY	4	11	18	25		2	9	16	23	30		6	13	20	27
FRIDAY	5	12	19	26		3	10	17	24	31		7	14	21	28
SATURDAY	6	13	20	27		4	11	18	25		1	8	15	22	29
SUNDAY	7	14	21	28		5	12	19	26		2	9	16	23	30

	JULY					AUGUST					SEPTEMBER				
MONDAY	1	8	15	22	29		5	12	19	26		2	9	16	23	30
TUESDAY	2	9	16	23	30		6	13	20	27		3	10	17	24
WEDNESDAY	3	10	17	24	31		7	14	21	28		4	11	18	25
THURSDAY	4	11	18	25		1	8	15	22	29		5	12	19	26
FRIDAY	5	12	19	26		2	9	16	23	30		6	13	20	27
SATURDAY	6	13	20	27		3	10	17	24	31		7	14	21	28
SUNDAY	7	14	21	28		4	11	18	25		1	8	15	22	29

	OCTOBER					NOVEMBER					DECEMBER				
MONDAY		7	14	21	28		4	11	18	25		2	9	16	23	30
TUESDAY	1	8	15	22	29		5	12	19	26		3	10	17	24	31
WEDNESDAY	2	9	16	23	30		6	13	20	27		4	11	18	25
THURSDAY	3	10	17	24	31		7	14	21	28		5	12	19	26
FRIDAY	4	11	18	25		1	8	15	22	29		6	13	20	27
SATURDAY	5	12	19	26		2	9	16	23	30		7	14	21	28
SUNDAY	6	13	20	27		3	10	17	24		1	8	15	22	29

Dear Carrie
In most countries of the world people drive on the right-hand side. Why is Britain different? When are you going to change?
Yours sincerely

Michel

Dear Michel
Yes, you're right, people drive on the right in *most* countries, but not all. They drive on the left in India, Pakistan, Bangladesh, Australia, New Zealand, Malaya and Thailand. Britain has more than 20 million cars and lorries. I know Sweden changed in 1967, but Britain is an island and it is not as important for us to change as it was for Sweden.

Carrie

2
Look at the calendar. Ask and answer questions, like this:
What's the date of the second Monday in August?

3
Fill in this questionnaire about yourself.
Then write a summary about yourself and your family.

A   PERSONAL DETAILS
Name: _____
Country: _____
Town: _____
Occupation: _____
Married/single: _____
Children: _____
Date of birth: _____

B   FAMILY DETAILS
Family members: _____
Occupations: _____
Ages: _____

C   INTERESTS
Languages: _____
Sports: _____
Books/films: _____
Other countries (travel): _____

D   YOUR PAST
School: _____
Past jobs: _____

E   YOUR FUTURE
Ambitions: _____
_____

42

4 Quiz

Write some words in your language under these headings:
fruit
vegetables
meat/fish
Only write words you do not know in English. Using dictionaries, ask and answer in pairs.
How do you say ____ in English?
Then write the English name next to the name in your language.

5

How good is your English? Listen to the tape to find out.

1 You are lost. You want to go to the station in an English town. What do you say?

2 You need help. What do you say?

3 You need to know the cost of something. How do you ask?

4 You want to know the distance from the post office to the station. How do you ask?

5 You want to know the weight of something. What do you say?

6 You want to know where someone went on holiday last year. What do you say?

7 You want to know how long the train takes between Hamburg and Hannover. What do you say?

8 Someone introduces his/her sister to you. What do you say?

9 Someone asks what you want to drink. How do you answer?

6

Here are some verbs from Units 37 to 41. What are they?

S_END   SL__P   E_RN

F__D   K_CK   W_TCH

Now complete these sentences.
1 Don't ____ a lot of money.
2 Do you ____ TV a lot.
3 I can't ____ her telephone number.
4 Some people ____ more money than others.
5 When you're tired you want to ____ .

7

How do you say these numbers in English? Listen to the tape to find out.

1 534–7856   6 8.55 pm
2 10,341   7 146
3 31st   8 2nd
4 111   9 11.15 am
5 709–4321

8 Crossword

The answers to this crossword are the opposites of the adjectives in the clues.

1 boring
2 empty
3 wide
4 new
5 thin
6 narrow
7 short
8 *Across* interested
   Down worst
9 loud
10 unpopular
11 happy
12 interesting
13 easy
14 small
15 dirty

A CHAMPION AT SIXTEEN

In the small Swiss town of Brig a young woman leaves a house at five o'clock every morning. For one hour she runs through the town and along the road by the woods. The young woman is sixteen-year-old Karin Meier, one of the best chess players in the world.

Karin is still at school, and has to study, like other people. But at home her life is very different. She gets up early and she never goes to bed late. In fact, she's usually in bed before nine o'clock. She gets up at five o'clock, goes for a run, then plays chess against her computer from six until seven o'clock. At seven she does yoga for half an hour, then she has breakfast and goes to school at 7.45. She sometimes sleeps in the afternoon.

Karin told us, 'In chess, like many other things, it's very difficult for a woman. No-one thought I could do well; my father wanted me to be a secretary!' In some ways Karin has a lonely life. She has few friends, and she's always thinking about chess. She told us, 'In my dreams I play chess. Sometimes I wake up and then I have to get up and play!'

1 Complete these sentences.
Karin ＿＿ at 5 o'clock.
She runs until ＿＿.
She plays chess from ＿＿.
She does yoga for ＿＿.
She sleeps ＿＿ hours.
She has ＿＿ at 7.30.
She goes to school at ＿＿.

2 In groups of four complete this table.

	A	B	C	D
What time do you go to bed?				
What time do you get up?				
How long do you sleep?				

Now ask questions of the other groups:
Who gets up the earliest/latest?
Who goes to bed the earliest/latest?
Who sleeps the most/least?
Answer like this: Peter, he gets up at ＿＿.

3 Karin's a chess player. It's an unusual occupation for a woman. Look at this list of occupations:

teacher	lorry driver	secretary
doctor	dentist	manager
nurse	architect	
tennis star	shopkeeper	

Now make three lists: jobs for men, jobs for women, jobs for both – and add more occupations.

4 Now compare your list with other people's.
Ask and answer.
Where have you put 'teacher'?
– Under _____.

5 Ask and answer in pairs.
What do you do?
– I'm a/I work in a _____.
Did you want to be a (job)?
– Yes, I did./No, I didn't.
What did you want to be when you were a child?
– I wanted _____.
What did your parents want you to be?
– They _____.

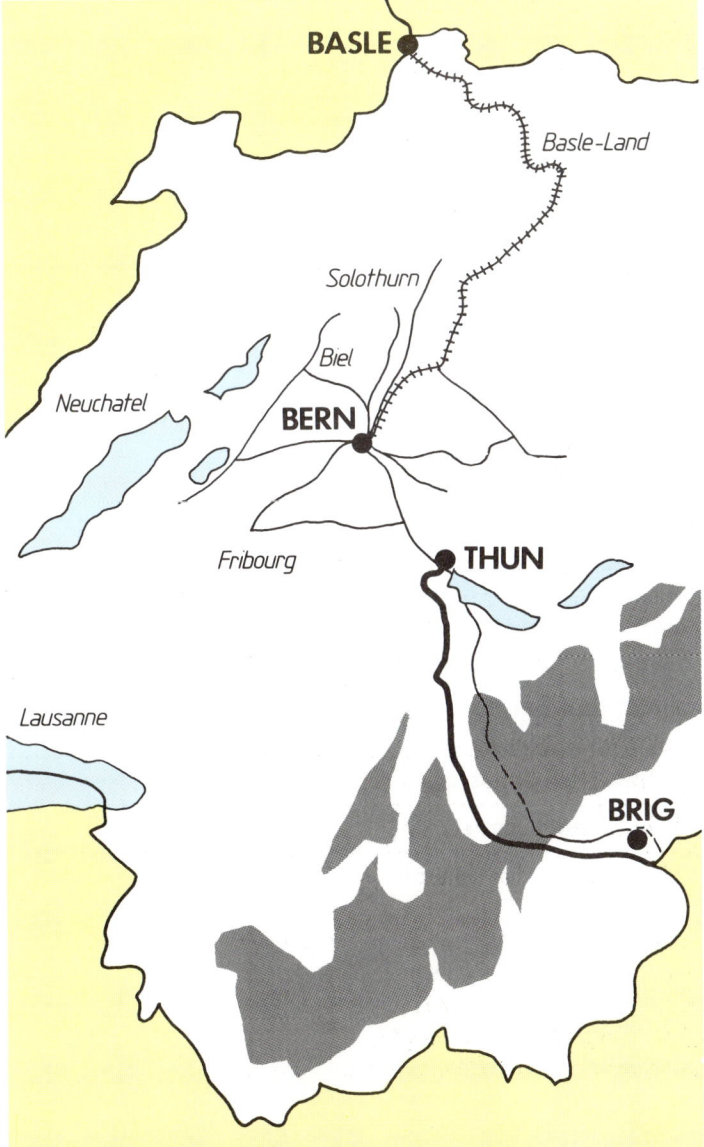

SUMMARY

Now you can :

talk about routines
talk about feelings

KEY GRAMMAR
Question forms
What time do you go to bed?
What time do you get up?
How long do you sleep?
When do you feel afraid?
What do you feel when . . .?

General statements.
At seven she does yoga for half an hour.
My father wanted me to be a secretary.
I feel afraid when I'm . . .

Prepositions	**Vocabulary**
along	prepare
through	want to be
until	win (won)

43

6 Listen to the tape. Next week Karin will play in the European Chess Championship.
How does she prepare for the Championship?
Use these verbs:
get up   run   play   eat   sleep

7 When do you feel lonely? (sad/afraid/worried/nervous/stressed/happy)
Say: *I feel _____ when _____.*
What do you feel when you want to eat? (drink/go to the doctor/take off your coat/sleep)
Say: *When I _____ I want to _____.*

8 Fill in the gaps with prepositions.
Use the map on the left to help you.

Last Tuesday Karin won the European Chess Championship _____ Basle. To get there, she left Brig _____ 6.30 am and travelled to Bern _____ car. She went _____ the mountains, _____ Lake Thun, _____ the town of Thun, then _____ Bern. _____ Bern she took the train _____ Basle. She arrived _____ Basle _____ 2.30 pm, so she travelled _____ eight hours.

91

CLIMBERS

When I have free time I go for a long walk. Some people read books or watch television. Other people play sports. Charles Mason and Linda Shaw do all of these things. They also climb buildings.

In the last five years they have climbed churches, office blocks and television towers. They have climbed in Paris, London, New York and Frankfurt. 'Other people climb mountains,' Charles told us, 'They climb them because they are there. We feel the same about buildings. When I see a building, a nice tall building, I want to climb. We climb everywhere, not only in the States. We've been to Europe many times.'

Two months ago the two Americans were in London. They visited the Houses of Parliament. 'When I saw Big Ben,' said Linda, 'I wanted to climb it straight away. But there were too many people around, so we waited, and that night, when it was quiet, we climbed up. Of course, the police didn't like it very much.'

Last month the couple were back in America. Two weeks ago police cars raced to the World Trade Centre in New York and traffic came to a stop. Charles and Linda were halfway up the building. When they came down the police arrested them. 'Buildings have lifts, don't they?' said one police officer. 'So why don't you use them?'

1 Answer these questions about the text.
Where are Charles and Linda from?
Where have they climbed?
What have they climbed?
What did they climb two months ago?
Where did the police arrest them?

2 Ask and answer in pairs.
What do you do in your free time?
– I watch television.
  (play sports, read books, go for a walk,
  listen to music, talk to friends . . .)
What else do you do?
How often do you do it?

3 Group survey
Work in groups of four and complete this table.

Have you ever . . . ?	A	B	C	D
climb/mountain				
be/abroad				
see/James Bond film				
see/film by Fassbinder				
read/book by Dickens				
be/in a sports car				
be/in hospital				
eat/Greek food				
eat/Chinese food				
eat/Indian food				
drink/sake				
drink/Irish whiskey				

4 Now write sentences about your group.
_____ has seen a James Bond film but _____'s never seen a film by Fassbinder. _____ has never eaten Greek food and has also never eaten _____._

5 Listen to the tape and fill in the gaps.

Interviewer Linda, what _____ in Paris now?
Linda Well, we love Paris, but we're really here because we're _____ climb the Montparnasse Tower.
Interviewer That's very dangerous, _____?
Linda Yes, it's very high, but we're not thinking about that!
Interviewer And the police won't like it. Have you _____ before?
Linda No, but _____ the Eiffel Tower.
Interviewer When _____ that?
Linda Oh, I think we _____ about two years ago, in winter, so there weren't many tourists.
Interviewer And what are you _____ next, after this?
Linda Have a glass of champagne!
Interviewer And then?
Linda Oh, I don't know. Maybe _____ return to America.
Interviewer And what are you going to climb next? _____ you tell me?
Linda Of course not. Wait and see!

6 Ask and answer in pairs.

Have you ever	been to Greece/Italy/India/South America?
	read a book by _____?
	seen a film called _____?
	visited Rome/Athens/Dublin/Hong Kong?
	eaten English/Japanese/Thai/Russian food?

No, I haven't. Yes, I have.	I	went to _____ in _____.
		read it _____ ago.
		saw it last week/month.
		visited _____ ago.
		have eaten _____ once/a few times.

7 You are a famous person, a film star, a sportsman or woman, a president perhaps. Now work in pairs, ask questions about your partner's person, and try to find out the name, like this:
Are you male or female?
Are you young or old?
Where did you live when you were young?
Where do you live now?
Are you an actor?
_Is your name _____?_

8 Now write about your partner's famous person.
_This man/woman is _____. He/she lived _____._

44

SUMMARY

Now you can:

talk about what you do in your free time.
talk about what you have and haven't done.

KEY GRAMMAR
Question forms
What do you do in your free time?
Have you ever seen a film by Fassbinder?
What are you doing in . . .?
What are you going to do next?

General statements
We've been to Europe many times.
She listens to music in her free time.
She's never read a book by Dickens.
I think we did it about two years ago.

Vocabulary
arrest
climb
race

TAWLEY
ARTS FESTIVAL
– another Cannes?

The Arts Festival at Tawley takes place every year, but it has not always been as large and important as it is today.

It started thirty years ago, when Tawley was just a small seaside town. The festival was very short that year, it only lasted two days. There were only two concerts – one in the evening of the first day, the other in the afternoon of the second day. For the two days the library became an art gallery for painters from Tawley! But there were very few visitors that year from abroad. Now the Tawley Festival is famous all over Europe. It continues for two weeks and Tawley has more than a hundred thousand visitors. It's still music and art but the cinema and theatre are becoming more and more important. In the next few years, the organisers of the festival will show many more new films and television programmes.

Jacques Martin, one of the French organisers, told us, 'In the next few years Tawley will be as important as Cannes for films and television. The weather is worse but the festival is going to be as good!'

1 Write six sentences about the Tawley Festival. Write two more about the past, two about now, and two about the future, like this:
Past: *The festival was very short thirty years ago.*
Present: *Tawley has more than a hundred thousand visitors during the festival.*
Future: *It will become more important.*

2 Look at the map and listen to the tape. Complete the key next to the map.

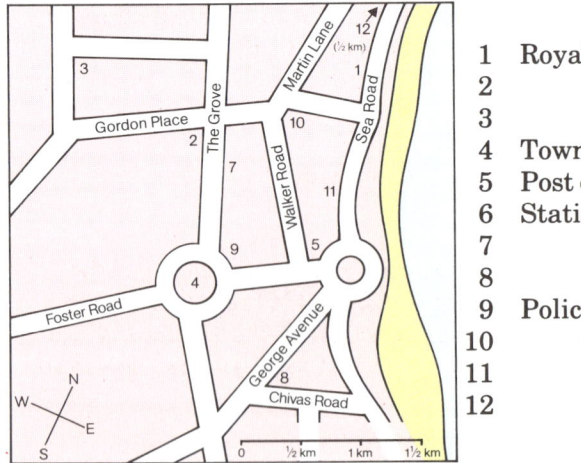

1 Royal Hotel
2
3
4 Town hall
5 Post office
6 Station
7
8
9 Police station
10
11
12

3 Choose a place on the map. Choose a second place or building. Where is it? How far is it from the first? Ask your partner questions like these:
How far is Gordon Place from George Avenue?
– It's about 1½ kilometres. It's next to the Albion Hotel.
How far is the small concert hall from the town?
– It's about ¾ kilometre, by the sea.
Does his/her answer agree with your answer?

4 Ask and answer in pairs.
How long does it take you to get from your house to the station? (post office, shops, cinema . . .)
– It takes me ____.
Where did you go yesterday? (last week . . .)
How long did it take?
How long did it take you to get here today?
– It took me ____.

5 Write about your town/village.
____ years ago ____ was ____. Now it is ____ and there is/are ____. Next year . . .
Write as much as you can.

PROGRAMME	JULY 18th		
		starts	ends
TV:	Children's programmes from France and Poland	10.00 a.m.	12.00 p.m.
Film:	*Comecomic* (An amusing look at life in Eastern Europe)	4.00 p.m.	7.00 p.m.
Music:	Mozart's *Piano Concerto in D Major* (and others) Pianist: Peter Fischer	7.15 p.m.	8.30 p.m.
Culture:	Rumanian Dances	8.00 p.m.	10.00 p.m.
Drama:	*King Lear* by Shakespeare	8.30 p.m.	11.30 p.m.

Some of these programmes are quite long. The film for example, lasts three hours. King Lear lasts two-and-a-half hours.

6 Ask and answer in pairs.
What time does/do ____ start/end?
How long does/do ____ last.

7 Work in pairs. You want to see something in the festival with your partner today (July 18th), but you don't know if he/she has enough free time. Look at your timetable for today and find out what you can see today.
Use: Let's go to ____.
    I can't because ____.
    That's a good idea.

A

Wednesday July 18th	
10.30 a.m.	Dentist
12.30 p.m.	Lunch with Sally, then shopping in afternoon
10.30 p.m.	Meet Peter for a drink

B

Wednesday July 18th	
10.30 a.m.	Hairdresser
3.00 p.m.	Tennis
6.30–7.30 p.m.	Piano lesson

SUMMARY

Now you can :

talk about programmes
talk about duration and distance

KEY GRAMMAR
Question forms
How far is Gordon Place from George Avenue?
How long did it take you to get here?
How long does it last?
What are you going to see?
What time does it start?

General statements
The film lasts 2½ hours.
It took me three hours.

Vocabulary
end
hear (heard)
last
take (with time)

45

8 Listen to the tape and fill in the gaps.
Who is Bob talking to?

Masters	Hello, My name's Bob Masters.
Fischer	Mine's Fischer, from Frankfurt.
Masters	What ____ in Tawley? Here for the festival?
Fischer	Yes. ____ some concerts and . . .
Masters	I see, so you ____. What are you going to hear? ____ a very good concert tonight. The pianist is a German. Fischel, I think.
Fischer	Fischer.
Masters	Ah yes. Are you going?
Fischer	Yes, I have to . . .

9 This year the Tawley Festival starts on July 14th and ends on July 27th. Complete the chart with details of festivals that you know. (eg wine, music, art . . .)

Name of festival	Type	Starts	Lasts
1			
2			
3			
4			
5			

TAPESCRIPT

1

3

Karl   Guten Tag. Ich heisse Karl. Darf ich mich hinsetzen?
Emma   I don't understand. Do you speak English?
Karl   Yes, I do. I'm Karl.
Emma   Are you German?
Karl   No, I'm not. I'm Swiss.
Emma   Where do you live?
Karl   I live in Zürich. What's your name?
Emma   I'm Emma.
Karl   Are you from England?
Emma   No, I'm not. I'm American.
Karl   Where do you live?
Emma   In New York.

2

2

The Orient-Express Competition. Answers.
Are you right or wrong?
A is from Paris. She's French.
B is from Milan. He's Italian.
C is from London. He's English.
D is from Lausanne. She's Swiss.
E is from Venice. He's Italian.

5

Rolf   Do you speak English?
Nicole   Yes, I do. But I'm French.
Rolf   Oh, do you live in Paris?
Nicole   Yes, I do.
Rolf   My name's Rolf.
Nicole   Hello. I'm Nicole. Where do you live?
Rolf   I'm from Hamburg, but I work in Düsseldorf.

3

1

Girl   Living Space.
Mr Baker   Hello. I'm from Blake's Hotel. I'd like some Supalux towels, please.
Girl   Yes, of course. What's your name, please?
Mr Baker   Mr Baker.

Girl	Mr Baker. And your address?
Mr Baker	Blake's Hotel, Brooke Street, London.
Girl	Blake's Hotel, Brooke Street, London. How do you spell Brooke?
Mr Baker	B-R-O-O-K-E.
Girl	B-R-O-O-K-E. Thank you.
Mr Baker	I'd like four red towels, two brown, three grey . . .
Girl	Four red, two brown, three grey . . .
Mr Baker	. . . ten orange, one yellow, one white . . .
Girl	. . . ten orange, one yellow, one white . . .
Mr Baker	. . . one green, five blue and nine black.
Girl	. . . one green, five blue and five black.
Mr Baker	No, nine black.
Girl	Nine black, right. Thank you, Mr Baker.

5 Listen to these words and write them down.

1	cupboard	*6*	armchair
2	picture	*7*	shelf
3	television	*8*	curtain
4	carpet	*9*	wall
5	light	*10*	window

4

1 This is Andrea. Today she's wearing a pink dress and white sandals. Her dress is from the Caravelle summer collection. She's carrying a white bag from Ecstasy.

This is Michel. He's wearing a pale blue shirt and dark blue trousers. He's carrying a grey jacket. His shoes are from Miracle.

And here's Janine. She isn't wearing holiday clothes this year. Today she's wearing a brown jacket and skirt, with a cream blouse and cream shoes. She's carrying a brown handbag.

Finally, Alexei is wearing trousers and a sweater by Lisko. His trousers are black and red and the sweater is purple and yellow. He's wearing a black hat, and is carrying a bag. Very colourful clothes!

8 Here comes number four. He's wearing a red cap and a red and yellow shirt, he's . . .
– In the blue corner is Dirty Dick, wearing the blue and white shorts.
– And today Susanna looks wonderful. She's wearing a lovely purple dress and white boots.
– The England team are wearing blue and white shirts, and white shorts.

5

4

Jennie	Hello.
Gabrielle	Hello, Jennie?
Jennie	Yes, this is Jennie. Who's speaking?
Gabrielle	It's Gabrielle. In Munich.
Jennie	Oh, Gabi! What's the time in Munich?
Gabrielle	It's twelve o'clock. What's the time in New York?
Jennie	It's six o'clock here. I'm getting up. Is Jürgen there?
Gabrielle	Yes, he is. He's having lunch.

5

Simon	Hello, Pilar?
Pilar	Yes, this is Pilar, who's speaking?
Simon	It's Simon. In Los Angeles.
Pilar	Oh, Simon! What's the time in Los Angeles?
Simon	It's one o'clock. What's the time in Madrid?
Pilar	It's nine o'clock here. Are you working?
Simon	No, I'm not. I'm having lunch. What are you doing?
Pilar	I'm having dinner.

7

1

Interviewer	Mrs Robinson. You live in Milton Keynes.
Mrs Robinson	Yes, that's right.
Interviewer	Do you live in a house or in a flat?
Mrs Robinson	I live in a house.
Interviewer	Is it an old house?
Mrs Robinson	No, it's new. Milton Keynes is all new.
Interviewer	Is it a large house?
Mrs Robinson	No, it's not very large.
Interviewer	How many bedrooms are there?
Mrs Robinson	There are three. Two large bedrooms and one small bedroom.
Interviewer	How large is the kitchen?
Mrs Robinson	I think it's eleven square metres.
Interviewer	Is there a garage?
Mrs Robinson	Yes, there is.
Interviewer	And do you like Milton Keynes?
Mrs Robinson	Yes, I do. I like it a lot.

TAPESCRIPT

7 I live in a semi-detached house, with three bedrooms, two living rooms, a kitchen and one bathroom. It's also got a large garden. The two living rooms are very large, and two of my bedrooms are also large, fifteen square metres, nine square metres and eight square metres, I think. The kitchen is ten square metres.

8

1

Reception	Hello.
Customer	Oh, hello. Have you got a room in July?
Reception	Yes, we have. For how many people?
Customer	Just my husband and me. Two people.
Reception	Do you want just bed and breakfast, or . . . ?
Customer	Is there full board?
Reception	No, only half board.
Customer	And how much does it cost?
Reception	It's £47 per person.
Customer	For one night?
Reception	Yes, and the two meals.
Customer	Thank you. And I also . . .

8

Tourist office	Hello. Minchhampton Tourist Office.
Customer	Hello, I want to stay in a hotel in Minchhampton.
Tourist office	Well, we've only got three, The Elm, the Hotel Placide and the Singing Fiddle.
Customer	How large are they?
Tourist office	The Elm has twenty rooms. The Hotel has thirty-five rooms and The Singing Fiddle has only eight rooms.
Customer	How much do they cost?
Tourist office	The Elm costs £16 per person a night. The Hotel costs £32 and the pub costs only £8.
Customer	Thank you, and what are the telephone numbers?
Tourist office	The Elm is 2-5-3-9-7, the Hotel is 6-0-7-4-4 and the Singing Fiddle is 8-1-6-6-0.
Customer	Thank you.

9

1

Interviewer	Isabella. You only have one week's holiday a year. When is it?
Isabella	My family has a baker's shop and I work very hard. My holiday is in February this year.

Interviewer	Tom and Alex. You work six days a week, and you work on Sunday. When is your day off?
Tom and Alex	Our day off is on Friday. We are working in Saudi Arabia, and nobody works on Friday there.
Interviewer	Mr Brown. You work over seventy hours a week. Where do you work?
Mr Brown	Oh, I've got a farm. I work very hard.
Interviewer	Carlotta, you work very hard. Why don't you have a holiday?
Carlotta	Because I've got eight children and I work very hard in the house.

10

1

1 – I'm John Robins. How do you do?
  – I'm Lise Braun. How do you do?
2 – Hello, Mary. How are you?
  – Fine thanks. How are you?
  – Very well, thanks.
3 – I'd like you to meet my sister, Jane.
  – Hello, Jane. Nice to meet you.
4 – Paula, this is my brother, Bob.
  – Hello, Bob. Pleased to meet you.
5 – Hello, everyone. I'm sorry I'm late.
  – That's all right.
6 – Hello, Mary. I'm sorry I'm late. Is that our train?
  – Yes, but it doesn't matter. How are you?
7 – I am sorry!
  – It doesn't matter.
8 – Thank you very much.
  – Don't mention it.
9 – I must go, Paula. Thank you very much.
  – It was nice to see you, John.
10 – I have to go now. Goodbye, father.
  – Goodbye, Richard.

4

1 Andrew, this is my sister, Julie.
  Don't mention it.
2 Hello, everyone. I'm sorry I'm late.
  It doesn't matter.
3 I must go now. Thank you very much.
  Hello, pleased to meet you.
4 Hello, Lisa, how are you?
  That's all right.
5 I have to go now, goodbye.
  I'm Louise Fletcher, how do you do?
6 Hello, how are you?
  It was nice to see you, Mick.

11

3

I'm Mary. My mother is Flory O'Grady. She is 101 and I'm 77. I've got eight daughters and two sons. I walk two or three kilometres every day and always drink a glass of Guinness at night. I never drink tea.

My name is Nikolai and I live in Georgia with my wife. All our family live a long time. I'm 105 years old and my wife is 103. Our two daughters are still alive. Our son is dead. I always eat garlic. I walk a lot and never sleep after five in the morning. I never eat meat.

13

1

Linda	Well, Paula, you exercise a lot, now what do you eat?
Paula	I eat a lot too, but I never eat any sugar. It's very bad for you.
Linda	What do you eat?
Paula	I always have some fruit for breakfast. An apple and an orange. And I eat a lot of vegetables.
Linda	What else do you eat? Do you eat meat?

Linda	Peter, how often do you exercise?
Peter	Well, I swim and run every day.
Linda	Now, tell me, what do you eat?
Peter	Well, I don't eat any meat. But I do eat fish and eggs.
Linda	Do you eat a lot of vegetables?
Peter	Oh yes, and fruit. I love fruit.
Linda	What do you drink?
Peter	Well, I never drink alcohol, coffee or tea. They're very bad for you.
Linda	What *do* you drink?
Peter	I drink a lot of milk. It's very good for you. I have milk and sugar with my cereal every morning.

14

5

Dr Lader talks about weight and height.
A lot of people are very heavy. Some are very fat. But there are also a lot of thin people. They are sometimes too thin. Very thin people and very fat people are often unhealthy.
– There is a good weight for your height, and your sex. A good weight for a man, for example, 1.8 m tall is 73·5 kg. A good weight ___

for a man only 1·6 m tall is 59 kg.
– A good weight for a woman 1·65 m tall is 60 kg. A good weight for a woman 1·5 m tall is 50 kg.

15

4

Interviewer	Heinrich, you do a lot of sports.
Heinrich	Yes, I exercise every day.
Interviewer	How many sports do you do?
Heinrich	Five.
Interviewer	And what are they?
Heinrich	Swimming, tennis, cycling, yoga and jogging.
Interviewer	Why do you like swimming?
Heinrich	Because it's good for the back and it's fun.
Interviewer	And cycling? What's cycling good for?
Heinrich	The legs. I like it because it's not expensive and I think it's relaxing.
Interviewer	You also do yoga.
Heinrich	Yes, that's right. Yoga's good for many things, but very good for breathing. It's also very relaxing.
Interviewer	But jogging isn't relaxing, is it?
Heinrich	No, it isn't. But it's good for losing weight and it's also very good for breathing. It's very good for the heart, too.
Interviewer	And tennis?
Heinrich	Yes, I like tennis very much. Tennis is fun, and sometimes it's very exciting. It's very good for the arms and legs. I like it a lot.
Interviewer	When do you go to work?
Heinrich	Oh, I work as well, but I have time in the evenings and . . .

16

3

It's Saturday morning in Bina, and on Saturdays hundreds of people come into the town to buy and sell. I've got a car here but there aren't many cars in the town. People come by riverboat and by bus. I've never been on a riverboat. They're very fast and cheap. The buses are crowded. I've never been on a bus here in Thailand – they're not very safe.

7

Interviewer	Mario, you travel a lot, don't you?
Mario	Oh yes, I travel by plane about twice a month. I'm an engineer now and . . .
Interviewer	But do you like planes.

Mario	No, I don't, I think they're dangerous, and they're very uncomfortable.
Interviewer	Teresa?
Teresa	Well I disagree, I don't think planes are dangerous at all. I like them a lot; they're fast and they're quite cheap. I travel a lot too, but by car. I really don't like cars, I think *they're* more dangerous than planes.
Interviewer	And what about you, Paolo?
Paolo	Well, I agree with Teresa, I don't like cars, I think they're very dangerous. In fact, I don't drive. But I travel a lot by train. Trains are safe and, in my country, they're very cheap.
Mario	Yes, but they're very dirty Paolo. I don't like them. And I disagree with you, Teresa, too. Cars are comfortable, fast, and I don't think they're very expensive.

17

1

A) Let's look at this car. It's small, smaller than a hatchback, but it's very fast. It's faster than a family car, and it's less expensive than a luxury car. It's a very good car.

B) This is a fantastic car! It's large and heavy, larger and heavier than a family car. It's cheaper than a luxury car and it's very safe. It's good for a family.

4

A	Oh, look at that sports car.
B	It's going too fast.
A	Have you ever been in a sports car?
B	No, I've never been in a car like that.
A	It's very safe.
B	Yes, but it's also very fast. I've never been in a sports car and I don't want to go in one.
A	Well, in my country people drive very fast. Have you ever been to Germany?
B	No. I've never been south of Dover.

9

Customer	Good morning. I want to buy a new car.
Assistant	What type of car do you want?
Customer	Well, I've got a small family, two children, and I don't drive very fast.
Assistant	Do you drive a lot?
Customer	No, not really. And I haven't got a lot of money. Really, I want a small, cheap, comfortable car.
Assistant	Well, I've got just the car for you. Look at this, It's fantastic. It's a hatchback. It's smaller and cheaper than a family car, and it doesn't use very much petrol. It's quite fast and it only costs . . .

19

1 Next time you fly, fly TOA. Toa has thirty flights a day from London to eight destinations. We have more early flights and night flights than any other small airline. We have eight morning flights, ten afternoon flights and seven late flights. Come to our four new, modern check-in counters and fly in our up-to-date planes, only six seats across with 80 cm leg room per passenger. Next time you fly, TOA wants to see you.

6 Welcome to TOA Flight NY 7 to New York. We are now serving drinks and dinner. Please look at your menus. Today we have fruit juice or soup for first course. The main course is chicken with fried rice, lasagne or steak with salad. For the dessert there is ice cream or apple pie, and to drink there is lager, wine or Coca-Cola. Enjoy your flight with TOA.

8 Listen to this survey.
A What is more important, better menus or cheaper flights?
B Cheaper flights.
A Better menus or more leg room?
B Leg room, I think.
A Better menus or fewer seats?
B That's easy, better menus.
A Better menus or better flight service?
B Mm, flight service, I think.
A And finally, better menus or more check-in counters?
B Oh, more check-in counters, definitely.
A Now, what do you think is more important, cheaper flights or more leg room?
B Cheaper flights.
A Cheaper flights or fewer seats?
B Cheaper flights.
A Cheaper flights or better flight service?
B Cheaper flights.
A Cheaper flights or more check-in counters?
B Cheaper flights, I haven't got a lot of money, you see.
A Now, what is more important, more leg room or fewer seats across?
B Er, more leg room, I think.
A More leg room or better flight service?
B Better flight service.
A More leg room or more check-in counters?
B More check-in counters.
A What is more important, fewer seats across or better flight service?
B Better flight service.
A Fewer seats or more check-in counters?
B Mm, more check-in counters, yes.
A And, last question, better flight service or more check-in counters?
B Oh, more check-in counters, definitely. Is that all, have I finished?

20

3 Part One

Interviewer	Roger, you lost your job. When was that?
Roger	Oh, I lost my job in the factory five years ago.
Interviewer	What did you do afterwards?
Roger	I was unemployed for a year. It was very bad. Then I went to night school. After that, I got a job in a bank.
Interviewer	And what do you do now?
Roger	Oh, I still work in the bank.

Part Two

Interviewer	Joan, what do you do now?
Joan	Well, I'm retired. I don't have a job. But I work hard in the house, and I work a lot in the garden.
Interviewer	Where did you work before?
Joan	I was a manager at Dobson's. I worked very hard. Then the factory closed. I worked in another factory for three years, and now I'm retired.

21

7

Detective	I want to ask you all some questions. You know that Consuela found a dead man here this morning. Someone killed him yesterday evening, they hit him with a bottle. Let's start with you Consuela. When did you find the dead man?
Consuela	At ten o'clock this morning, in his room.
Detective	Where were you yesterday evening?
Consuela	I was at the disco with Joe.
Detective	OK, good. Now, Pierre, where were you yesterday evening?
Pierre	I was in the kitchen all evening.
Detective	Who was with you?
Pierre	Manuel. He was in the dining room, but he came into the kitchen at ten o'clock for his dinner.
Detective	Mm. Now, Molly, where were you?
Molly	I was at the reception desk until nine o'clock, then I walked into the town with Pedro. We had a drink.
Detective	Who's Pedro?
Molly	Manuel's brother.
Detective	Whose brother?
Molly	Manuel's. He's staying with Manuel. He came back to the hotel at ten o'clock, but I stayed in the town.
Detective	Thank you Molly. Now, Manuel, you were in the kitchen with Pierre yesterday evening?
Manuel	Yes, after work.
Detective	What about Pedro, where was he?
Manuel	With Molly, she just . . .
Detective	After that.

Manuel   I don't know. I didn't see him until midnight, in our room, he was in bed. He didn't want to talk.
Detective   Why is he here?
Manuel   Well, he's looking for work. You see, he's been in prison in Spain and there's no work for him there . . .

22

5

A   Oh, look at these two watches, aren't they lovely?
B   Which one do you like?
A   They're both very nice. I think I like . . .
B   Do you like this one?
A   Mm, yes, but I think I like that one better. It's made of gold, isn't it? And look at these rings! Now, they're lovely.
B   Mm, I don't know, I think I like those better, over there, the plain gold ones.
A   But these are gold, they're white gold.
B   Look, which one do you like?
A   I think I like that one. Do you want to buy it for me?

23

5

A   Have you ever been to Britain on holiday?
B   Oh, yes, I've often been to Britain.
A   Where have you been?
B   Well, last year we went to the Lake District, but we've also been to Scotland and Ireland. We always go in summer because the weather is better.
A   Yes, but there are more tourists.
B   Yes, that's right. But it's the same in every country.

25

5

Caller   Hello, is that Photofax?
Photofax   Yes, it is.
Caller   Can I speak to the repair man please?
Photofax   What's your name?
Caller   David Roscoe.

Photofax   Can you spell that, please?
Caller   R-O-S-C-O-E.
Photofax   And what's your address?
Caller   35, Tanner Street, London, EC15.
Photofax   And your telephone number?
Caller   246 8071.
Photofax   246 8071. What's the serial number of your machine?
Caller   The number is XY 307841.
Photofax   Thank you very much, Mr Roscoe. Which signs are on?
Caller   The red triangle.
Photofax   Is the red repairman on?
Caller   No, but the rectangle is on.
Photofax   I see. Have you turned the machine off yet.
Caller   No, I haven't.
Photofax   Turn it off now, don't use it . . .

26

7 At first it was very difficult. Caroline helped me a lot. After the accident I couldn't do anything. I was in bed, I couldn't move. I couldn't help in the house. For six months Caroline stayed at home with me.

Now, it's better. I have a special car and I can drive. We have a special house and I can help in the house. I can cook. I can't do sports any more, but I can still teach.

9 I come from India, I'm a Hindu. I can eat vegetables and fruit but I can't eat meat. I don't eat beef because the cow is very important to Hindus.

I come from Saudi Arabia, I'm a Muslim. I can't eat any meat from a pig; I can't eat pork, ham and bacon. I can eat all vegetables and fruit and I can drink milk, but I can't drink any alcohol.

I come from China, I'm a Buddhist. I'm a vegetarian; that means I can't eat any meat or fish, but I can eat vegetables and fruit, and I can drink alcohol.

27

9

Woman   Please, can you help me? I'm very worried, I can't find my . . .
Policewoman   Just sit down, madam. Now, what's the problem?

Woman	It's my daughter. I can't find her anywhere. Oh I'm so terribly . . .
Policewoman	Your daughter. How old is she?
Woman	Seven. Just seven.
Policewoman	Where did you last see her?
Woman	Outside the post office. I went to the post office. I went inside, just for a minute, and when I came out she wasn't there.
Policewoman	What is she wearing?
Woman	A blue dress. It's new, I bought it for her birthday. Yes, it's a blue dress, with a black jacket, and black shoes. She's got long brown hair. Oh, she looks like me; everyone says she looks like me. Oh, yes, here, look . . . I've got a photograph, look. Please help me.
Policeman	All right.
Man's voice in background	. . . we're looking for a young girl, aged seven, last seen near the post office. She's wearing a blue dress, with a black jacket . . .

28

1

Anna	I was born on a train in Hungary.
Caspar	On a train?
Anna	Yes, it's true. My poor mother. She was on her way to Budapest, to my grandmother's house. It was early in the morning on the sixth of January, 193_, but you don't want to know the year, do you?
Caspar	So, you grew up in Hungary?
Anna	Yes and no. I lived in Hungary for five years, and then I went to school in Paris. My father was a singer, and my mother played the piano. Oh, she played the piano very well. And in Paris I met my first husband.
Caspar	Was he French?
Anna	No, that was my third husband.

4

Anna couldn't do anything. My English was very bad, but Anna's was worse. She couldn't shop, she couldn't take a bus, she couldn't use the phone. And, of course, in London people come from all over the world. One day, there was a Chinese gentleman at the door. 'Marie-Chantal', she said. 'Tell him I don't speak Chinese.' 'But Anna,' I told her, 'he's speaking English.'

29

3

A	Hello, London Information Service. Can I help you?
B	Yes, I'd like to see the Lord Mayor's Parade. What time does it start?
A	It starts at ten past eleven, from London Wall.
B	Where does it go?

A   It goes to the Mansion House, St Paul's, The Guildhall and other places.

B   How do I get to The Guildhall from Blackfriars underground station, please?

A   Go up New Bridge Street until you come to Ludgate Circus. Turn right at Ludgate Circus and walk past St Paul's. When you are on Cheapside turn left into Wood Street. Walk up Wood Street until you come to Gresham Street on your right. Go down Gresham Street, and The Guildhall is on your left.

B   Thank you. How far is The Guildhall from Blackfriars?

A   It's about a kilometre.

B   And how long does it take?

A   About ten minutes, or quarter of an hour.

31

9

Woman	Hello, how are you?
Man	Fine thanks. And you?
Woman	Oh, not so bad. Come into the kitchen.
Man	Thank you.
Woman	Take a seat. Would you like a cup of tea?
Man	Yes, that would be nice.
Woman	Or perhaps you'd prefer coffee?
Man	No, I'd like tea, please.
Woman	Well, the kettle's just boiling. Do you take milk?
Man	No, thank you. Can I have lemon?
Woman	Oh, I don't know if I . . . wait a minute . . . yes, here's a lemon. Sugar?
Man	Yes please.
Woman	How many?
Man	Two please.
Woman	Right, here you are.
Man	Oh, that looks lovely, thanks.

32

8

A   Hello, operator. I'd like to call Brazil. When is the best time?

B   The cheapest times are before eight in the morning, after six at night, or at the weekends.

A   You mean it's more expensive at the moment?

B   Yes, before midday is the most expensive time.

A   What time is it now in Sao Paulo?

B   Well, it's 11.00 a.m. here, so it's 8.00 a.m. there.

A   All right, I'll wait till nine tonight.

B   Yes, that's probably best.

33

8 Robert is being interviewed for the radio.

Interviewer Robert. You're not a young man. Why did you go on this journey?
Robert Oh, for many reasons. I love Britain but I also love travelling.
Interviewer Why don't you travel around Britain?
Robert Well, I know Britain quite well, and I love the countryside, but I find English food very boring. I like foreign food. Also, the hotels are very expensive and not very good – they're much better in France, for example.
Interviewer So you don't like very much about Britain.
Robert Oh, I do. I love the people; they're so friendly; and I think our television's also very good. But, you know, one of the most important things to me is the weather.
Interviewer The weather?
Robert Yes, I hate the weather. I like the British summer, it's often quite good, but the spring is often very wet.
Interviewer Yes, but in the winter it's not very cold. And we don't have much snow.
Robert That's right, but it rains a lot. I like the sun. I've always liked the sun so I certainly don't like the British winter.

34

2

Barratt Here, doggie, come on boy.
Old man Excuse me, sir. Can you help me?
Barratt Certainly. What's wrong?
Old man Well, my car's broken down. I'm a doctor and I'm in a great hurry. I must return to the hospital at once.
Barratt What can I do? How can I help you?
Old man I must get a taxi, but I've left my money at the hospital. Can you possibly lend me some?
Barratt Well, all right. Is five pounds enough?
Old man Can you give me ten pounds? Give me your address and I'll return it to you tomorrow.

35

2 1 I never go out of the house. I stay inside. I only see my husband and children. I never go shopping. I never go into the street. I like my own room. I feel safe there.

2   Yesterday I went up in a lift. I wanted to go up to the twelfth floor but on the fourth floor six people got in, and on the seventh floor four more got in. The lift was too full and I felt very hot. I wanted to get out. I got out at the tenth floor and walked up the stairs. Then I felt better.

3   I'm all right in an aeroplane. In fact, I really like flying. But I feel very frightened in tall buildings. I can't look out of the windows at all. Yesterday I went with a friend to a restaurant at the top of a very tall building. We sat near the window and I felt really sick. I couldn't eat anything.

7

Doctor	Hello, Mrs Charles. Come in and sit down.
Woman	Hello, doctor.
Doctor	What's the matter?
Woman	I've got backache.
Doctor	Do you often have backache?
Woman	No, I don't. I've never had a bad one before.
Doctor	When did it start?
Woman	About four days ago.
Doctor	Well, go home and rest in bed for two days, then you'll feel better.
Woman	Can you give me some medicine? It's very painful.
Doctor	Yes, I'll give you some pills. Take one three times a day, and come back in three days. If you don't feel . . .

37

10

Interviewer	Your name is also James Houseman. Is that right?
James	Yes, it is. I'm named after my grandfather.
Interviewer	And you go to the same school.
James	Yes, my grandfather was here eighty years ago.
Interviewer	What's it like? Is it very different now?
James	No, I don't think so!
Interviewer	What are the rooms like? How many boys sleep in your room?
James	Twenty.
Interviewer	And is the room warm in winter now?
James	No, it's very cold all the time!
Interviewer	What do you eat for breakfast these days?
James	Well, we have a good breakfast. We have cereal to start . . .
Interviewer	Hot?
James	No, cold, you know, like cornflakes. Um, then we have a hot course, you know, eggs, bacon, sausages, tomatoes, that sort of thing . . .
Interviewer	Any mushrooms?
James	Sometimes, yes. Oh, and we also have toast and marmalade, and tea, of course. I think it's quite a good breakfast really.

38

5

Waiter	Good evening. Menu?
Man	Ah. Thank you.
Woman	Mm, look at this. I love doner kebab, it's my favourite.
Waiter	Are you ready to order?
Man	Yes, I think so. Mm, what are you going to have to start?
Woman	I think I'll have houmous.
Man	And I'll have squid.
Waiter	I'm sorry. We haven't got squid today.
Man	Oh, I see. I'll have houmous as well then.
Waiter	Very good. Your main course?
Woman	I think I'll have a doner kebab with a mixed salad.
Man	Mm, I think I'll have yoghurt kebab.
Waiter	With a salad?
Man	No, I don't think so.
Waiter	To drink?
Man	Oh, I think, er, a bottle of white wine?
Woman	Yes, that's lovely.
Waiter	Would you like to order your dessert now?
Man	Oh no, we'll wait till later, thank you.

39

5

A	Where are you going on holiday this year?
B	I don't know yet. I'm thinking about Spain.
A	I'm going to Spain.
B	Are you? When?
A	In August. Let's go together. Spain's lovely, you'll like it.
B	Oh, that's a nice idea. I've already been to Spain. I love the food, and the beaches are super!
A	Have you ever been to Cresta?
B	No, I've heard about it, but I haven't been there yet. Actually, I wanted to go there last year, but I couldn't. I was ill.
A	Oh, that's a shame. But let's go this year, we can visit Barcelona, too.
B	Oh yes! I've already been to Barcelona but I'd love to go again. It's very hot and crowded, of course, but there are lots of lovely shops and we can . . .

10

Officer	Now, all these five hotels have swimming pools . . .
Tourist	Oh good, er, what about beaches?
Officer	Well, only the first two have private beaches, the Winter Garden and the Stella Maris are both next to the beach, but the Summer Palace is in the centre of town.
Tourist	Ah, well, that's not so good, is it? What about the restaurants, I'm

very interested in good food.

Officer Let me see, mm, well, I think you'd like both the Beauregard and the Stella, they've got excellent restaurants. The Four Seasons doesn't have one, the Summer Palace has quite a good restaurant, but, personally I don't like the Winter Garden's restaurant.

Tourist Now, um, how expensive are they? I can't spend a lot.

Officer I'm afraid the Beauregard is very expensive, more than fifty pounds a night.

Tourist Oh dear, I'll forget that one.

Officer Now, the Winter Garden and the Summer Palace are both about thirty pounds, the Stella Maris is a little cheaper at twenty a night and the Four Seasons is about twelve.

Tourist So, it's the Beauregard 50, the Four Seasons 12, the Winter Garden and the Summer Palace 30, and the Stella Maris 20.

Officer That's right.

Tourist Now, I'd like their telephone numbers . . .

Officer All of them?

Tourist Um, perhaps not, just give me the numbers of the Winter Garden, the Summer Palace and the Stella Maris.

Officer Right, the Winter Garden is 98512, the Summer Palace is 99321 and the Stella is 92783.

Tourist Right, thank you very much indeed. Goodbye.

40

4

Man . . . and what are you reading now?

Woman A book called 'Winter and Summer'

Man Oh, I haven't read that one yet. Who's it by?

Woman The author's F. Y. Peters. Do you want to read it after me?

Man Oh, I don't know. Is it a romance? You know I don't like them much.

Woman No, it's an adventure. I think you'll like it. Look. I have another book here, by Caroline Dick, do you want to read that? I've already finished it.

Man No, thanks. I'm reading an interesting book at the moment. I'd like to finish it first.

Woman Oh, what is it?

Man It's called 2010, you've probably heard of the first book, that was called 2001.

Woman Oh yes, I do know that. Is it science fiction?

Man And adventure, with a little bit of romance. But yes, you're right, it's really science fiction.

Woman What's it about?

Man It's about a man called Heywood Floyd and a computer, that's called HAL 9000 and . . .

Woman Who's it by?

Man Arthur C Clarke.

Woman Is it good?

Man Yes, it's very exciting.

Woman It's not frightening?

Man No, not at all.

7

What are you reading now?	A book called 2010.
Who's it by?	The author's Arthur C Clarke.
Is it a romance?	No, it's a science fiction story.
What's it about?	It's about a computer and ...
Is it good?	Yes, it's very exciting.

41

1

Are these sentences true or false?
1 Global Studios are spending a lot of money on their latest film.
2 The film takes place in Europe.
3 George Castle is in Spain now.
4 George Castle has finished filming.
5 It's an adventure story.
6 Hannibal is Robert West's fifteenth film.

2

George Castle is directing a scene from Hannibal.

Director Right, let's get ready now. Robert, you're going to walk from the right, so you wait by the rocks, OK? Now, Inge, you're already on the set, you're sitting next to the pond, brushing your hair. Is that OK? That's right, relax a bit, good. Jennifer, I'm afraid you're not in this scene, my dear, so just come back here, next to me, no, not in front of the camera, you fool! Louis, you're in the right place, that's right, stand between the two large tents, good, and Roy, you come in later, from the left, so just come and stand behind the small tents, that's right, just by the stream. OK, are we ready? Let's go!

42

5

1 Excuse me, how do I get to the station?
2 Can you help me, please?
3 How much does this cost?
4 How far is it from the post office to the station?
5 How much does this weigh?
6 Where did you go on holiday last year?
7 How long does the train take from Hamburg to Hannover?
8 Pleased to meet you.
9 I'd like a cup of tea, please.

7
1 five three four, seven eight five six
2 ten thousand, three hundred and forty-one
3 thirty-first
4 one hundred and eleven
5 seven oh nine, four three two one
6 five to nine
7 one hundred and forty-six
8 second
9 quarter past eleven

43

6

Interviewer	How do you feel, Karin, are you nervous?
Karin	Yes, very, but I run every morning and then I feel better.
Interviewer	How far do you run in the morning?
Karin	Oh, usually about eight kilometres, but sometimes I run more than that, when I feel very nervous.
Interviewer	How do you prepare for the Championship?
Karin	Well, the running, of course. I eat very little and I sleep a lot.
Interviewer	But you get up very early, then you run and play chess against your computer, don't you?
Karin	Yes, but I'm going to bed earlier now.
Interviewer	So how long do you sleep each night now, just before the championship?
Karin	I try to sleep for nine or ten hours a night, and sometimes I sleep in the afternoon.
Interviewer	Are you going to win, Karin.
Karin	Oh yes, of course I'm going to win!

44

5

We talked to Linda in Paris recently.

Interviewer	Linda, what are you doing in Paris now?
Linda	Well, we love Paris, but we're really here because we're going to climb the Montparnasse Tower.
Interviewer	That's very dangerous, isn't it?
Linda	Yes, it's very high, but we're not thinking about that!
Interviewer	And the police won't like it. Have you ever climbed it before?
Linda	No, but we've climbed the Eiffel Tower.
Interviewer	When did you climb that?
Linda	Oh, I think we did it about two years ago, in winter, so there weren't many tourists.
Interviewer	And what are you going to do next, after this?

Linda	Have a glass of champagne!
Interviewer	And then!
Linda	Oh, I don't know. Maybe we'll return to America.
Interviewer	And what are you going to climb next? Won't you tell me?
Linda	Of course not. Wait and see!

45

2 Welcome to the Tawley Arts Festival. Look at the map of Tawley in front of you, and I'll tell you how to find places in the town. You are at the Town Hall; that's number four on the map. North from here you can see a long road called The Grove; on the right of The Grove is the theatre, and on the left, on the corner of Gordon Place is the Albion Hotel. Some of the films will be in this hotel. On the other side of Gordon Place, the north-west corner, is the Walsh Gallery. If you look east from where you are now, the Town Hall, you can see the sea, but in front of the sea there is a very large building; that's the Main Concert Hall. It's on the corner of George Avenue and Chivas Road. On Sea Road, just north of the post office you'll find the new cinema, where you can see most of the films. The town museum is to the north-east, on the corner of Walker Road and Martin Lane; there's an exhibition called 'The History of Television' here. Finally, the Small Concert Hall is just outside the town, about half a kilometre north of the Royal Hotel.

8 Bob meets Fischer in a pub in Tawley.

Masters	Hello, my name's Bob Masters.
Fischer	Mine's Fischer, from Frankfurt.
Masters	What are you doing in Tawley? Here for the festival?
Fischer	Yes. There are some concerts and . . .
Masters	I see, so you like music. What are you going to hear? There's a very good concert tonight. The pianist is a German. Fischel, I think.
Fischer	Fischer.
Masters	Ah yes. Are you going?
Fischer	Yes, I have to . . .

CONTENTS REVIEW

	Structures and lexical fields	Life skills	Exponents	Recycling
1	Present simple – 1st person singular – 2nd person singular – with question words Question words – *what?* – *where?* Short forms Possessives – *your*	Introducing yourself Talking about nationality	I live in Zürich. I'm Swiss. Are you American? Do you speak English? What's your name? Where do you live? Where do people speak English? Yes, I am./No, I'm not. Yes, I do./No, I don't. What's your name?	
2	Present simple – 3rd person singular (*he/she*) – 3rd person plural (*they*) – with question words Question word – *what language?* Short forms	Asking and answering about nationality Asking and answering about language Asking and answering about home towns	He/she's from Paris. He/she speaks French. He/she lives in Paris. He/she's Swiss. Where does the winner live? What languages does he speak? Yes, he is./No, he isn't.	*Where?* *I do./I don't.*
3	Present simple – 3rd person singular (*it*) Question words – *what?* – *how?* Colours Numbers 1–10 Articles *a/an*	Spelling Counting Asking the name of objects Asking about colour	It's a bed. It's blue. What is a . . . in English? How do you spell . . . ?	*I'm . . .* Question words – *What's your name?*
4	Present simple – 3rd person singular negative and interrogative – with question word and noun – with complement (eg adjective) Short forms Present continuous – 1st, 2nd, 3rd person singular Possessives – *his/her my* Articles – *the*	Talking about clothes	What colour is her skirt? The jacket is brown. She isn't wearing holiday clothes. Is Andrea wearing a skirt? Yes, it is. No, it isn't.	*Yes, he is.* *No, he isn't.* Colours
5	Present simple – for everyday actions Time prepositions Place prepositions Question words – *who?* Present continuous – with question word *who?*	Saying what you do every day Saying what other people are doing now Telling the time	She doesn't have .dinner at home. She has her breakfast at 7.00 am. It's half past six. What's the time in Los Angeles? Who's speaking? Is Jürgen there? In Singapore Lucy Wu is having dinner. What is Jennie doing?	Present continuous Present simple Possessives – *his/ her my*

Analysis of review units follows Unit 45.

	Structures and lexical fields	Life skills	Exponents	Recycling
7	*There is/are* Present simple – with *have got* – with question words Question words – *how many?* – *how large?* Numbers 11–20	Talking about houses	There are three rooms. Is there a garage? Yes, there is. No, there isn't. How many rooms has it got? How large is your bathroom?	Short forms – *I do/don't.* – *It is/it isn't.* Numbers Possessives
8	Present simple – 1st, 2nd, 3rd person plural (*we, you, they*) Question word – *how much?* Short forms Prepositions *want* Numbers	Talking about hotels and flats Talking about prices	It costs . . . How much does it cost? Have you got a . . .? It costs over £5. We've got a room. How many beds are there in the . . .? Yes, we have.	*There is/are* Present simple + *have got* Possessives – *your*

9	Question words
	– *when?*
	– *why?*
	– *how long?*
	Because
	Possessives – *'s*
	   their our
	Days and months
		Talking about holidays
		– when
		– length
			When is your day off?
			Why doesn't she have a holiday?
			. . . because she's got eight children.
			How long is your holiday?
			Their holiday is in February.
				Question words
				– *who?*
				   have got
				Possessives – *my/your*

10	All formulae as under life skills *He's my . . .* *This is . . .* *I'd like you to . . .*	Introducing yourself and others Apologising Thanking Saying goodbye	How are you? Sorry I'm late. Thank you very much. I have to go now.	
11	Present simple – with adverbs of frequency (*always never*) Question words – *how old?* *any* Family members	Saying how old people are Talking about your family	He always eats garlic. She never eats any sugar. How old are you? How many sisters have you got? Have you got any brothers?	Possessives – *my our* Present simple + *have got*
13	*some/any* Question word: *how often?* Short forms *a lot of* *good/bad for one*	Talking about what you eat Talking about how often you exercise	I always have some fruit. I never eat any sugar. I don't eat any fruit. Do you eat any fruit? How often do you exercise? Milk is good for you.	*any* Present simple + *always never*

	Structures and lexical fields	Life skills	Exponents	Recycling

14	Comparatives
	– *-er than . . .*
	– *more/less than . . .*
	Question words – *how tall/heavy?*
	Adverbs – *too*
	     quite
	     very
	     only
	Object pronouns –
	  me you
		Talking about weight and height	He is taller than me.
			Do you weigh more or less than the average?
			How tall/heavy are you?
				how often?
				a lot of
				there is . . .

15	Present simple – short form *and so is . . .* – with question words *(very) few* *as well* *too* Adjectives	Talking about sports Using numbers Saying why you like something	Jogging is good for your heart and so is tennis. Why do you like . . .? I work, as well. It's good for the heart, too.	*is good for . . .* *only . . .* *why . . .? because . . .?* *how many?* *how often?*
16	*It's* + adjective Present perfect – with *never ever* Comparatives – *more* *less* } *. . . than* Prepositions	Talking about travel Saying how often you do things	It's easy. He's never been on a boat. Trains are more dangerous than planes. I travel by plane twice a month. Has the old man ever been on a boat?	Present simple *why . . .? because . . .?* Question word – *how?* *too* *lots of* *some*
17	Question words – *which?* Replacive pronouns – *one* Adverbs	Comparing (cars)	Which car is larger, A or B? I don't want to go in one. Do you like it a lot? It's going too fast.	Comparison Present perfect with *never ever* *How much/many/old?*
19	Comparatives – *more/fewer/less . . . than* – *better/worse* *I'd like. Would you like?* *What* as subject of a question. *but*	Comparing and giving reasons Ordering a meal	ACB is good, but TOA is better because . . . What would you like? The main course is . . .	Comparatives Present simple Question words – *which?* – *what?*
20	Past simple – all persons – with question words – with *ago* – with regular verbs – with *be, lose* *ago/next/now* Present perfect Occupations	Talking about your job now Talking about your job in the past	What was Jean? She was a manager. What happened five years ago? She lost her job. What happened next? Have you changed your job in the last five years? Where did you work before?	Present perfect

CONTENTS REVIEW

CONTENTS REVIEW

	Structures and lexical fields	Life skills	Exponents	Recycling
29	Imperatives for directions Present simple with *take* Prepositions of place Question words – *how long?*	Asking for and giving directions	Turn right. Where is the Guildhall? How do I get to Blackfriars? How long does it take? It takes about ten minutes.	Comparatives Question words – *when?* – *how long?* – *how?* – *where?* Occupations
31	Imperatives for instructions *either . . . or* *-ing* forms connectors – *first next and finally then*	Sequencing actions Saying what you prefer to drink	Boil the water, then warm the teapot. What do French people like drinking? Do you prefer tea or coffee? I like either tea or coffee.	Imperatives Question words Present simple *is from*
32	Superlatives – *the* + adjective + *-est* – *most/least* + adjective – *best/worst* Replacive *do* in the past	Using superlatives	Which . . . is the best value? Before midday is the most expensive time. Milk costs twice as much now as it did ten years ago. Supermarket A's tea is the cheapest.	Comparatives Past simple Question words – *which?* – *when?* The time
33	Past simple – with question words – for narrative – with irregular verbs Adverbs Connectives of sequence – *after before* *nobody*	Talking about the weather. Talking about travelling.	What was the weather like? How long did it take? He travelled slowly After Paris he went through . . .	Present perfect Question words – *what?* – *how long?* Connectives – *then next* etc. *conjunctions* Likes and dislikes *take* + time *too quite very*
34	Future – *will* (preview) Past simple – with *when* clauses Direct object pronouns – *you me him/her it them us*	Describing people Borrowing things (money)	Is five pounds enough? Can you lend me some money? When will you return it?	Present perfect Past simple for narrative Present continuous *want* *look like* *nobody no one* *when* clauses
35	Gerund as noun *afraid of . . .* *frightened of . . .*	Asking for and giving advice Talking about fears	Are you afraid of flying? Flying is less dangerous than travelling by ship.	Comparatives *because . . .* Imperatives *can/could* *best*
37	Future – *will* – *going to*	Making plans Talking about the future	I'm going to tell my father. John Bennett will publish the book.	Past simple for narrative *will* as future *feel* + adjective Days and months Types of food *why . . . ? because . . .* Sequencing

	Structures and lexical fields	Life skills	Exponents	Recycling
38	Possessive pronouns – *mine yours hers his theirs ours*	Talking about restaurants – eating in a restaurant Comparing 'yours' and 'ours'	Mine was good but hers was better.	*going to* future *will* future Past simple + *ago* Comparatives and superlatives Present perfect Names of food
39	Present perfect – with *already* and *yet* warnings – *be careful of* *Let's* + verb	Talking about things you've already done, or haven't done yet	Have you been to Cresta yet? I've already been there. Let's go to . . .	Past simple Present perfect *very/quite/not very* + adjective Adjectives *must* *can/couldn't*
40	Replacive pronouns – *one it* Adjectives *will* as recommendation/promise	Talking about interests – books	Who's it by? Which kind of fiction do you like best? Have you read this one yet? You'll like it.	Question forms Present perfect with *already* and *yet* Adjectives Stating preferences
41	General revision Adverbs – *rarely often* Prepositions of place	Talking about interests – films	How often do you go to the cinema? She doesn't go very often. It's near the station.	Comparatives Superlatives Comparing past and present Prepositions Imperatives
43	General revision *When* clauses Question words *want someone to do something*	Talking about routines Talking about feelings	What did you want to be? . . . when you were a child . . . My father wanted me to be a secretary.	Superlatives *feel* + adjective Prepositions
44	General revision Past simple with question words Present perfect with question words Present perfect with *ever*	Talking about your free time	What do you do in your free time? What did they do two months ago? Have you ever read a book by Dickens?	Present perfect
45	General revision	Talking about interests – festivals	How long did it take you to get here? What time does it start? What are you going to see?	Prepositions *because* . . . Directions *take* + time

122

	Recycling	Activities
6	What language do people speak in . . . ? Where do you . . . ?　　　I live/work in . . . What's your . . . ?　　　My . . . . What time do you . . . ?　　　I get up at . . . . What colour is the . . . ?　　　It's . . . . What's the time?　　　It's	Letter writing Recognising verbs Pair work: interviews Pair work: Asking about colours 　　　　　　Asking how to spell words Unscrambling words, and making sentences
12	Socialising formulae from Unit 10 How many + plural nouns There are . . . How large is your kitchen/bathroom/ 　garden etc? Calendars/dates Family members: Who is . . .'s son/ 　daughter etc? How much does . . . . cost?	Letter writing Matching captions to cartoons Recognising verbs Family tree Quiz Pair work Completing a calendar
18	Have you ever been to . . . ? Some diets are good and some are bad. I haven't got any . . . Which person is heavier? A is more expensive than B. There aren't many . . . in column A. How do you say . . . . in English?	Letter writing Matching text and visuals Pair work Sentence writing Recognising verbs Crossword
24	When she lived in Nice she was at school. She wasn't at school twelve years ago. What time did you get up? What did you have for breakfast? Jürgen is a doctor and he works in a hospital. . . . is the same as . . . . . . is larger than . . . Which train takes longer, the . . . or the . . . ?	Letter writing True/false Pair work Guessing games Recognising verb forms Completing sentences Puzzle
30	I can . . . , but I can't . . . Open questions A is the same as B because . . . I look like . . . Which month was . . . born in? How old is . . . ?	Letter writing Reading comprehension Puzzles Conversation corner Recognising verbs
36	. . . is smaller than . . . . . . is the lightest . . . The weather in London today is cloudy and 　quite cold. Which travels slowly? What do you feel like when . . . ?	Letter writing Quiz (adjectives/feeling) Making sentences about the weather Recognising verbs Unscrambling words Crossword
42	How do you say . . . in English? Asking questions (survival English). Saying numbers.	Letter writing Completing a questionnaire Quiz Recognising verbs Crossword (adjectives)

INDEX

This index gives the unit number of the first occurrence of each word.

ACKNOWLEDGEMENTS

The publishers would like to thank the following for their co-operation in the production of this book:

Photographs and information pages 8 and 9 courtesy of *Venice Simplon Orient-Express Ltd.*

Relyon Ltd for the multi-purpose furniture on page 10.

Milton Keynes Development Corporation for information and permission to reproduce the black and white photographs on pages 18/19.

Barclays Hotel Group for kind permission to use one of their hotels on pages 46/47.

Beales Department Store, Walton-on-Thames, for the loan of the objects on page 49.

Pat Tramacco for the photographs on pages 60/61.

Acropolis Restaurant, Walton-on-Thames, for the photographs on page 80.

Photographs

The publishers would like to thank the following for kind permission to reproduce copyright photographs:

Zefa for pages 6, 14 (baker), 15 (farmer), 20 (Edinburgh), 52 (hospitals) and 82 (all photographs).

Camerapix Hutchinson for pages 8 (A,B,C,D), 36 (man on motorbike, girl in boat), 50/51 and 83.

The Design Council for page 11 (top).

Elizabeth Whiting for page 11 (bottom).

Sporting Pics for page 15 (tennis player).

Terry Gross for pages 18/19 (Milton Keynes).

Tony Stone Associates for page 20 (St Ives, Exeter and London), 52 (doctor), 66 (tea taster) and 75 (mouse, dog, spider and bull).

The Image Bank for page 8(E), 22 (engineers, Carlotta), 58 (George, Geoff and Julia Brown), 59 (all photographs), 64, 72 and 73 (businesswoman and cook).

Barnaby's Picture Library for page 26 (old ladies), 27 (Korean man) and 36 (bus, boy, woman with children, station).

The Photo Source for page 27 (Georgian man).

Jane Munro for pages 29, 35, 41, 66 (glasses) and 68.

Imag for page 36 (man with bicycle).

Citröen Cars Ltd, Ford Motor Company Ltd, British Leyland PLC, Peugeot-Talbot Ltd, Austin-Rover and *Porsche Cars Great Britain Ltd* for pages 38 and 39.

Slimming Magazine for page 40.

The Sunday Times for page 58 (Richard Darwin Keynes).

The Mansell Collection for page 58 (Charles Darwin).

Mary Ann Kennedy for pages 62 and 63.

The Tea Council for pages 66 (man in bed) and 67 (tea drinkers in street).

The Daily Telegraph Colour Library for page 73 (doctor and student), page 75 (frog, snake and bat), page 93 (Eiffel Tower) and 94 (World Trade Centre).

O S Films for page 75 (cockroach).

Giggleswick School for page 78.

Clive Barda for page 94 (pianist).

Donald Cooper, London for page 94 (King Lear).

C M Dixon for page 94 (Rumanian Dancers).

Design

Jo Harris and Karen Osborne for creative design
Carol McCleeve for camera-ready paste-up

Front Cover – Dancewear supplied by The Dance Centre, Covent Garden, London